Institution

Institution

Roberto Esposito

Translated by Zakiya Hanafi

polity

Originally published in Italian as *Istituzione* © 2021 by Società editrice Il Mulino, Bologna.

This English edition © Polity Press, 2022

This work has been translated with the support of the Center for Books and Reading of the Italian Ministry of Culture.

Polity Press
65 Bridge Street
Cambridge CB2 1UR, UK

Polity Press
101 Station Landing
Suite 300
Medford, MA 02155, USA

ISBN-13: 978-1-5095-5155-2
ISBN-13: 978-1-5095-5156-9 (paperback)

A catalogue record for this book is available from the British Library.
Library of Congress Control Number: 2021950727

Typeset in 11 on 14 pt Sabon
by Cheshire Typesetting Ltd, Cuddington, Cheshire
Printed and bound in Great Britain by CPI Group (UK) Ltd, Croydon

The publisher has used its best endeavors to ensure that the URLs for external websites referred to in this book are correct and active at the time of going to press. However, the publisher has no responsibility for the websites and can make no guarantee that a site will remain live or that the content is or will remain appropriate.

Every effort has been made to trace all copyright holders, but if any have been overlooked the publisher will be pleased to include any necessary credits in any subsequent reprint or edition.

For further information on Polity, visit our website:
politybooks.com

Contents

Translator's Note   vii

By Way of a Prologue   1
I.   The Eclipse   5
II.   The Return   23
III.   The Productivity of the Negative   39
IV.   Beyond the State   56
V.   Institutions and Biopolitics   76
Epilogue   96

Notes   100
Index   110

Les institutions sont la garantie du gouvernement d'un peuple libre contre la corruption des mœurs, et la garantie du peuple et du citoyen contre la corruption du gouvernement

Institutions are the guarantee of a free people's government against the corruption of morals, and the people's and citizens' guarantee against the corruption of the government.

Louis Antoine de Saint-Just

Translator's Note

Regarding the Italian *costituente*, *destituente*, and *istituente*: these words could be translated, using the present participle, as *constituting*, *destituting*, and *instituting*. The result is ambiguous, though: for example, is "instituting thought" an action or a way of thinking? To avoid this confusion, in agreement with the author, I have chosen to follow the paradigm of *constituent power*.

This usage has a long history in English translations of political philosophy from French (*pouvoir constituant*), Italian (*potere costituente*), and German (*verfassungsgebende Gewalt*). It also reflects the use of "constituent power" in a large corpus of scholarly works on the topic written originally in English, from Hannah Arendt's *On Revolution* (1963) to Lucia Rubinelli's *Constituent Power: A History* (2020).

While perhaps more distant from everyday language, "instituent thought" maintains its close genealogical kinship with the concepts and history out of which it arises.

Zakiya Hanafi

By Way of a Prologue

"Vitam instituere"/To Institute Life

In an obscure but crucial nook of the Western tradition, the expression *vitam instituere*, to institute life, poses a still unresolved question. At the heart of this phrase, which Humanist tradition linked to a text by a Roman jurist named Marcianus, stands the enigmatic relationship between institution and human life. We must resist the persistent temptation to view them as diverging poles, destined to meet up, or collide, only at a certain moment. Rather, they should be recognized as the two sides of a single figure that delineates at the same time the vital character of institutions and the institutent power of life. What else is life, after all, if not a continuous institution, a capacity for self-regeneration along new and unexplored paths? This is what Hannah Arendt meant when she said that human beings constantly start something new because, being born into the world, they themselves are a beginning.[1]

This first beginning was followed by another, the

faculty of speech, which we can regard as a second birth. From that came cities – the political life that opened the horizon of history, although without ever cutting the thread that binds it to its biological roots. However different the regime of *nomos* may be from that of *bios*, it has never separated from it. If anything, their relationship has become tighter and tighter, to the point that it is impossible today to talk about "politics" without mentioning life. Institutions are at the center of this shift. They are the bridge by means of which law and politics shape societies, differentiating and uniting them.

This is why, even in the most dramatic circumstances, we can never stop instituting life and redefining its contours and objectives, or its conflicts and opportunities: because human beings are instituted by life, which ushers them into a common world, inseparable from the symbols that express it over time. This symbolic dimension shapes people no less than it is shaped by them, and it is not something added to human life from the outside: it makes human life what it is, distinguishing it from all other types.

No human life is reducible to pure survival – to "bare life," to use Walter Benjamin's well-known expression. There is always a point at which life projects out beyond primary needs, entering the realm of desires and choices, passions and projects. Given that human life has always been instituted, it never coincides with mere biological matter – even when crushed, by nature or history, and flattened into its hardest stratum. Even then, for as long as life is such, it reveals a way of being that, however deformed, violated, or trampled upon, remains what it is: a form of life. It receives this quality by belonging to a historical context made of social, political, and cultural relations. That which institutes us from the beginning, and which we ourselves institute continuously, is a web of relations within which the things we do acquire meaning for us, but for others too.

Of course, all this is predicated on the condition of staying alive. The unfolding of the relational life presupposes the staying power of the biological life, the possibility of survival. There is nothing reductive about the word "survival": although vivid in our hopes and fears today, it is etched deeply into the entire history of humankind. The issue of *conservatio vitae*, the preservation of life, has been central to classical and modern culture. It resonates in the Christian appeal to the sacredness of life as well as in the political philosophy introduced by Hobbes, and touches the raw nerves of contemporary biopolitics. Staying alive is the first task demanded of individuals in every society: a challenge not always won and, indeed, regularly lost, that looms up again from time to time with unexpected violence.

This defensive act precedes all other options; it is their precondition and prerequisite. But after the first life, and along with it, we must also defend the second life, the one that is instituted and has the capacity to institute. For this reason, staying alive requires that we not give up on the other life, our life with others, tied to the most powerful meaning of *communitas*. This applies to both the horizontal plane of society and the vertical line of generations. The primary task of institutions is to allow a social ensemble to live together in a given territory, but also to ensure continuity throughout change, by extending the lives of parents into those of their children. The meaning of *institutio vitae*, the institution of life, must

---

be traced in part to this necessity. Even before fulfilling a functional use, institutions respond to humans' need to project something of themselves beyond their own lives – beyond their own deaths – by extending their first birth, so to speak, into their second.

I
The Eclipse

From the Pandemic

The coronavirus pandemic threatened to tear this dense fabric apart with unexpected violence. Much has been written about the phenomenology of the pandemic, with intentions and arguments that need not be repeated here. Our attention is better focused on the relationship between the emergence of the virus and the response of institutions. If we can shift our gaze away from the very deep wounds that the pandemic has inflicted on the body of the world, the task that now awaits us is to institute life anew or, more ambitiously, to institute a new life. The urgency of this need takes precedence over any other economic, social, or political necessity, because it forms the material and symbolic horizon from which all the others derive their meaning. After being challenged and at times overwhelmed for months by death, life seems to be calling for an instituent principle to restore its intensity and vigor.

But this cannot be done without first asking a

fundamental question about the way institutions responded to the challenge of the virus, particularly in Italy. To keep a balanced judgment, we must guard against generalizations, by distinguishing between and articulating different levels of discourse. Certainly, negative aspects abound in the efforts that regional, national, and international institutions made to contain the damage; so much so that the negative can even be said to have prevailed at times over the positive. It is impossible to forget the inadequacies, shortages, and delays of the early interventions, which sometimes caused irreparable social harms and, especially in some areas, health harms as well. This lack of decisiveness was sometimes accompanied by excess intrusion into individual lifestyles, even when not strictly required, adding substantial political, economic, and social costs. The shifting of boundaries between legislative and executive powers in favor of the latter, caused by the use of emergency declarations that were not always necessary and sometimes arbitrary, went so far as to threaten the democratic endurance of political systems. These appeared to be struggling in the inevitably failed attempt to pursue and match the effectiveness of the more drastic procedures implemented by authoritarian regimes. In the second wave of the pandemic, still in progress at the time of writing, miscalculations and failures to act have been even more evident, with effects we will be able to gauge in the coming months; not to mention the horrific number of victims in Italy, higher than in comparable European countries.

Even so, it behooves us to ask about the role of institutions in reverse terms: How would we have withstood the virus's onslaught without institutions? What would have happened, in Italy and elsewhere, if there had been no institutional framework to guide our behavior? Looked at from this point of view, it must be acknowledged that the contribution of institutions appeared for quite some time to be the only available resource. I am referring not only to regional and national administrations but to all institutions in the areas affected by the virus – from social organizations and professional associations to non-governmental organizations (NGOs) – which have represented the last line of resistance against the pandemic. The fact that the virus did not engulf all barriers and spread undisturbed is owed essentially to them.

No doubt, as has been said, we acted in a state of emergency and, therefore, although the two concepts cannot be superimposed, in a state of exception with respect to institutional normality. But, leaving that aside for the moment, it was a state that could not be extended indefinitely and was later legitimized by the Italian Parliament. Most importantly, it was provoked not by a sovereign will to extend control over our lives but, rather, by a mix of necessity and contingency that was completely unforeseeable and quite different from a project aimed at subjugating the population. As legal scholars know, necessity is one of the primary sources of law, along with custom and written laws. In the case in question, the role of a tragic contingency is clear, with the consequent need to contain it. Certainly, for those who have the power to proclaim a state of emergency and prepare a response, the decision is always subjective. But in this case one is hard pressed to deny the degree of objectivity of an event whose beginnings and effects have very little of the voluntary or planned about them.

Similarly, it is undeniable that, in our intensely bio-political regimes, healthcare has become a directly political matter at the disquieting crossroads between the politicization of medicine and the medicalization of politics; just as it is evident that our awareness of health has significantly increased compared to any previous type of society. But this, it seems to me, is not a bad thing. The fact that the right to life is considered an unquestionable premise on which all others are based marks an achievement of civilization from which we cannot retreat. In any case, our current biopolitical regime should not be confused with a system centered around sovereignty, because it constitutes a profound alteration of that system. Imagining that we are at the mercy of an unlimited power intent on taking over our lives does not account for the fact that centralized decision-making has long exploded into countless fragments, largely autonomous from national governments and located even in a transnational space.

Well then, keeping in mind all the limits mentioned above, it can be said that, on the whole, institutions in Italy withstood the impact of the disease, activating their immune antibodies. Of course, we know that every immune reaction, if intensified beyond a certain threshold, risks provoking an autoimmune disease. This happens when a society is overly exposed to desocialization. The problem our political systems always face is that of finding a sustainable equilibrium between community and immunity, between the protection and compression of life. The strength, but also the adaptability, of institutions is measured by how well they are able to adjust their defense level to the threat at hand while not underestimating or amplifying its perception.

During the early stage of the pandemic, institutions were hit by controversies arising from perspectives often so diametrically opposed that they canceled each other out. Institutions were criticized for doing too much and for not doing enough, due to indecision. Accused by some of unlawfully curbing individual liberties, to others they seemed incapable of governing individual and collective behaviors with a firm hand. Needless to say, as far as these kinds of criticisms are concerned, I have no intention of questioning their legitimacy or, as regards several of them, their merits, both of which seem well founded. But we must not lose sight of the fact that even the harshest criticism of institutions can only be developed from within them. What else are the media, websites, newspapers, and even writing and language, if not also institutions? True, they are different from political institutions and sometimes in blatant opposition to them. After all, conflict is not extraneous to democratic institutions; indeed, it is a prerequisite for their functioning.

The logic of the institution – or rather of what in this book I will call "instituent praxis" – implies a continual tension between inside and outside. Whatever lies outside institutions, before being institutionalized itself, alters the previous institutional structure, challenging, expanding, and deforming it. The difficulty of recognizing these dialectics stems from two mistaken assumptions that form the polemical objective of this book: the tendency to equate all institutions with state institutions; and the tendency to view them as static, as "states," instead of in continuous becoming. As the masters of legal institutionalism teach, not only do there exist extra-state institutions but also anti-state institutions, such as protest movements that possess some form of organization. They express an instituent energy that institutions should also keep alive in order to "mobilize" and, in some ways, surpass themselves.

Institutions and Movements

This two-fold need for institutionalization and mobilization was obscured especially between the 1960s and 1970s, with the gradual rise of a rigid opposition between institutions and movements. If we take a broad look at the debate over the last few decades, we see it split into two apparently unreconcilable poles, in radical opposition to each another. On the one hand, there is a renewed proposal for a conservative model of institution, resistant to any transformation; on the other, a proliferation of anti-institutional movements that are irreducible to the unity of a common project. The result of this divide has been an increasingly stark disconnection between politics and society. An institutional logic closed in on itself, incapable of speaking to the social world, is opposed by a scattering of different protests, incapable of melding into a politically incisive front.

Symptomatic of this difficulty, at once theoretical and practical, has been the counterproductive outcome of both tendencies. Just as the self-referential closure of institutions has provoked a reaction of drastically anti-institutional attitudes, these in their turn have led institutions to further rigidify. With all intermediate terms excluded as a matter of principle, conservative institutions and anti-institutional practices have reinforced each other, blocking any political dialectics of renewal. Very few have managed to resist this binary logic by attempting a discourse capable of integrating institutional endurance and social change.

Even Michel Foucault, who applied his formidable genealogical thought to critiquing the apparatuses of confinement and psychiatry, assumes a closed, repressive notion of institution. Not surprisingly, he views "sequestration" as the generative paradigm of every institutional *dispositif*. Despite the incomparable analytical potential of Foucault's work, it ultimately puts forward an idea of "institution" not too distant from the "total institution" theorized during the same period by Erving Goffman. Unlike Franco Basaglia – who directed his critique to a specific type of mental institution and helped to dismantle it[1] – Foucault tended to characterize all institutions as oppressive. For him, taken together, they constitute a solid block destined to confine life within guarded and rigidly divided spaces, compressing natural instincts and tendencies.

Despite presenting a wealth of productive hermeneutic insights, Foucault's perspective must be inscribed in an interpretive framework that is shared widely by a broad array of intellectuals. During those years, albeit with opposing intentions, right- and left-wing authors converged in this closed, defensive notion of the institution: the former, to reinforce it; the latter, to challenge and ultimately demolish it. When we read side by side the writings of authors like Sartre, Marcuse, and Bourdieu on the one hand and Schmitt and Gehlen on the other, it is easy to discern a subtle shared agreement on a static, inhibiting interpretation of institution.

For cultural sociologists Peter Berger and Thomas Luckmann, in a different argumentative framework, institutions are artificial *dispositifs* necessary to order natural tendencies by selecting them. The basic idea that inspires these analyses is that human nature, left to itself, would end up self-destructing. At its origin – along a vector that runs from one side to the radical left of Herbert Marcuse, and from the other to the ethological right of Konrad Lorenz – lies Freud's thesis of civilization as an inhibition of primary drives. For Freud, "civilization" defines the set of institutions that differentiate our life from that of animals, serving the dual purpose of protecting us from nature and regulating our relationships with others.

Institutions, which the patricidal brothers in *Totem and Taboo* introject in place of their dead father, embody powers, wield commands, and impose penalties without which human society would implode. Therefore, says Freud, we must adapt to the "discontent" that civilization causes and ultimately sacrifice part of our freedom to it; to the point of viewing institutions as a sort of automatic thought pilot, as Mary Douglas writes in a book entitled, appropriately, *How Institutions Think*.[2] Although they are created by us, they take on a second nature, more rigid than the first, that precludes any possibility of criticism. Starting with the strongest and most established institution, that of the state, they are at once the system of rules that govern the community and the power that enforces adherence to that system.

Naturally, such a coercive interpretation of institutions has provoked an equally radical anti-institutional response from those who contest their legitimacy, leading to the progressive consolidation of a radical front still active today. If the institution is by its nature reactionary, all that remains is to fight it head-on, without the need for too many distinctions. The armed conflict of the 1970s in Italy was the extreme outcome of this perspective, blocked by the incapacity to think of institutions and movements together. Its strategic failure produced a further step, which did not, however, modify its anti-institutional tone. Once the frontal charge against institutions had failed, the other avenue taken by the philosophical left, as early as the 1990s, was that of disabling them. This is the theory that has recently taken the name of "destituent power," whose watchwords, ringing with a faint Heideggerian echo, are "withdrawal," "abandonment," and "exodus."

The resumption today of explicitly anarchic stances follows the same line of argumentation, alternating between revolutionary calls for constituent power and appeals to destituent power. What connects them, albeit in opposition, is a demand for immediacy that opposes any institutional mediation. According to a radically anthropological vision, what must be liberated is the fluidity of a social relationship no longer filtered by the political. It is the immediacy of the relationship that really counts. Along this line of thinking, an authentic community is not qualified by its social bond but by its disintegration. The political or, better yet, the "impolitical" outcomes of this reasoning are plain for all to see today.

The Invention of Nature

It would be highly reductive, however, to confine the difficulty of thinking innovatively about the paradigm of institution to political debate over the last fifty years. The problem began much longer ago, before modernity itself, with its early roots going back to the

Christian conception of medieval canonists and glossators. Although they proclaimed themselves heirs to the ancient Roman jurists, they marked a real turning point with respect to the way the Romans used the idea of "institution." The latter had applied a verb form to the term, applied to a huge category of individuals. Thus, the people who were instituted, in the sense of "nominated" or "commanded" could be administrators, procurators, heirs, priests, and so forth.

Examined from our point of view, this verbal quality of *instituere*, compared to the noun *institutio*, assumes strategic importance, because it gives the concept a dynamic tone that projects it beyond the static dimension it would later acquire. In the remarkable wealth of Roman juridical texts, *istituire* ('to institute') meant not only to establish particular situations but also to produce them artificially, on the basis of requirements that arose over time. It was Yan Thomas, the brilliant historian of Roman law, who mainly emphasized this "operative" attitude of Roman law.[3] Its instituent character expanded to the point of embracing the very foundation of Rome. But even more curious is the fact that the idea of "nature" itself was instituted; that is, it was used artificially for specific purposes. In an essay entitled "L'institution de la nature" (The institution of nature), Thomas detects a genuine reversal of the relationship between institution and nature. Instead of nature being conditioned by the law, binding it to values contained in nature, Roman law used the idea of "nature" for its own purposes.

Obviously, this mode of action presupposes a prior operation of denaturing *ius*. Roman law is never subordinated to principles that transcend its sphere of action.

It is always free to transgress them: as with the institution of slavery, which was declared *contra naturam* (against nature) by the jurists themselves. Of course, there is a line beyond which the law cannot cross. But this is a physical or biological limit: for example, a father cannot be younger than his son, just as a woman cannot produce an unlimited number of offspring in the same pregnancy; whereas incest, which is possible in nature, is prohibited by law. It is not nature, in short, but the law that establishes what is doable or not doable within objective boundaries that circumscribe human experience.

But the law's autonomy from all natural principles does not stop here. Not only can it disregard nature, but it can use nature for unnatural purposes. The Roman jurists' instrumental use of the concept of "nature" for their various purposes is striking, starting from an issue that was particularly delicate in Rome: the freeing of a slave. To free a slave from his or her servile condition, the law appeals to the natural state of human beings, which it itself violated when it instituted slavery. In this way, an unnatural condition – that of the slave – is abolished through fictitious recourse to a natural principle of equality. Thus, nature is contradicted twice: first by making a naturally free human being into a slave, and then by freeing that person via instrumental reference to a natural canon. Simply put, the unnatural power of the law goes so far as to use natural protocols against itself. In this way, it makes nature the instrument of institution, and institution the presupposition of nature.

This denaturalization procedure is what the Christian authors contested. Not only did they restore the intangibility of nature but also the legitimizing role that the law had removed from it. The relationship between institution and nature was thus doubly modified. Furthermore, in the twilight of the Roman Empire, nature was no longer considered available to the operations of law, and even became its insuperable constraint. Instead of law instituting nature, nature instituted law, in a form that gave new meaning to the concept of "natural law." The law no longer legislated on the basis of nature but, on the contrary, conformed to it, giving voice to the law contained within nature. This is where the Christian canonists brought about a real paradigm shift with respect to the Roman jurists: they made a clean break in their definition of "nature," which was now given and no longer instituted.

Rather than breaking all relations between nature and institution, however, the Christian writers reconfigured it by inserting a third element, that of God, between them, thereby changing both. The fact that nature is "given" does not mean, in fact, that it is eternal, as in Greek philosophy, but that it has been "given" to creatures by the Creator. This way, instead of the instituent principle disappearing, it is transferred from the sphere of law to that of theology. Nature is unavailable to the law because it is literally in the hands of a *Deus institutor*. From this perspective, even the idea of "instituting life" undergoes a semantic conversion, placing a gap between the two terms that is destined to transform them both. Instead of being self-produced, life is instituted by a divine will that precedes all other institutions. This leads to a drastic change in the relationship between the natural given and the instituent power. Every institution is put on a metaphysical horizon that makes its nature a divine creation.

This dialectic is recognizable in all its severity in Augustine's *City of God*, whose frontal attack against Rome, central to the work – especially against Marcus Terentius Varro and Cicero, considered its greatest ideologists – played a crucial role in the construction of Christian political theology. At stake is none other than the subject of institution. In book six of *The City of God*, Augustine locates Varro's error in having considered things instituted by humans as divine. The foundation of this sacrilege, he says, is specifically the reversal of the relationship between history and nature, which corresponds to that between humans and gods. Any concept that places the earthly city before that of God destines it for decay.

In the momentous transition represented by Augustine, the Roman juridical paradigm collapses. In its place there arises a new idea of "institution": that which institutes life is neither law nor the history of humans but, on the contrary, their obedience to the God who originally instituted them, who is the sole master of justice. Law can be defined as "natural" on condition that nature be considered the work of God. Likewise, evil is not forbidden because it is evil, but because it is forbidden by God. This theological turning point was destined to efface the Roman-derived *institutio vitae* for at least a thousand years. From a possible subject of instituent praxis, life now returns to being a passive object of an institution that is entirely dependent on the sovereign will of whoever holds its keys.

Institution

Sovereign Institutions

The model of institution that spread in medieval history was strongly affected by this shift in tone from a functional dimension, as was the Roman, to an authoritarian mode with a transcendental character. This shift took place in parallel with the semantic transition from the category of *persona*, pertinent to the individual, to that of a *ficta* (fictitious) or *repraesentata* (represented) person introduced by Sinibaldo Fieschi (Pope Innocent IV), referring to non-human entities, such as universities or monasteries, that enjoy specific prerogatives.[4] This turn is notable for its top-down character, evident when comparing the notions of corporation and foundation: whereas the corporation is expressed in the will of its members gathered in the *collegium*, and the foundation is dedicated to the preservation of a collective good, the institution is distinguished by an authoritarian element in force not only at the time of its birth but also throughout its lifespan.[5]

This authoritarian tone remains engrained in the concept of "institution" for a long time. From then on, even in its secularized version, institution has continued to evoke a power established once and for all, a repetitive mode of its particular way of being and functioning. What prevails in the concept of "institution" is a sort of reiteration removed from history and rigidified in the fixity of an eternal present. The instituted – its predetermined, irrevocable outcome – predominates over the instituent. During the Middle Ages, although the concept of "institution" did not refer to a state body, which was still in the process of forming, *institutio* did refer intensively to what has been (*stato*) or established (*stabilito*). It invoked the permanent quality of history rather than its constituent moment.

This withdrawal from historicity is crucial for how "institution" would be reshaped in modern political culture. To allow the power it expresses to shine forth in all its plenitude, two things had to be erased from memory: the process that produced it and, even more so, its often-violent origins. The founding, instituent moment goes missing, now absorbed entirely into the established, instituted moment.[6] This is how the product of a praxis that is artificial – historically determined – was assimilated into a given of nature, corresponding in its turn to the will of God, of which *institutio* is an earthly expression. Institution is what allows a power to endure in time without being called into question by its members.

The Ancien Régime gave even more emphasis, if that is possible, to this hierarchical assumption, incorporating it into the monocratic figure of the absolute sovereign. Over the course of time, the king's law prevailed so strongly over all other statutes, customs, and habits that it canceled out, or deprived of importance, the very word "institution." It is often accompanied or replaced by others that emphasize its stability, such as the French *établissement*. In reality, the noun *institutio*, or *institutum*, does not disappear completely, but it normally refers to the sovereign: to the set of rules with which he must comply in order to fulfill his duty as a good Christian and model for the faithful. Accordingly, the sovereign, placed at the head of the institution, is himself the *institutor* (founder, organizer, or originator), engaged in the institution and instruction that ensure civil, religious, and military order. Missing from the idea of "institution," at least until the beginning of the eighteenth century, is any reference to the impersonal mechanisms into which the governmental administration is condensed – an administration too subordinate to the sovereign power to be able to assume an independent form and its own denomination. Although often used interchangeably in juridical treatises of the period, a deep rift continued to separate the static notion of *institutio* from the dynamic one of *constitutio*, a breach that was destined to pass into modern constitutions. As the historian of institutions Alain Guéry observes, what makes their use problematic is the fact that absolute monarchy is not conceived as instituted but rather as proclaimed by divine right.[7] For this reason, it cannot be thought of in terms of "institution." The state is the "statute" of the kingdom, embodied sacredly in the person of the king, who is located at the connection point of his two bodies, one mortal, the other dynastic. King and kingdom cannot be thought of separately until the administrative structure of the state acquires autonomy and reconfigures the institutional lexicon. *Institutio* is none other than the sacred tie binding man to God at the point of intersection between time and eternity.

This history came to an end, or was radically changed, during the French Revolution. In the final period of the Ancien Régime, something similar to an administrative system began to take form in some ways externally to the sovereign will, because it necessarily entertained relationships with organizations, powers, and interests not entirely represented by the monarchy. This was a first perceptible shift toward the modern concept of "institution." Used at first negatively – for example, in the French constitution of 1791, to define the orders of nobles and medieval corporations that were being abolished – it began to take hold bit by bit as the complex of bodies in which the social and political life of a country is expressed. The contrast alone between the new constitutional regimes and the pre-revolutionary one signals the shifting, differentiated character of political institutions.

And yet, this was not enough to steer institutional logic toward dynamism and cause the emergence of an instituent praxis. For a long time to come an authoritative element lingered, despite the transition from the medieval tradition to modern political philosophy. Even Hobbes, despite a dramatically renewed conceptual horizon, reproduces both the personal character of the Leviathan state and the absoluteness of its power. He uses the word "institution" to refer indifferently to the state, government, and sovereignty. These varied meanings already emancipated the concept from the theological leaning of canon law and introduced it into a new domain. The very idea of a Hobbesian "social contract" draws attention to the origin of the institution in a form far removed from Christian creationism. Still, the Leviathan state incorporates every other institution within itself, subordinating them to its own absolute command – which is why institutional thinking dried up: although empowered, it was also entirely absorbed into the monopoly of the state.

Although with different intents and conceptual tools, not surprisingly, 250 years later both Max Weber and Carl Schmitt reproduced what Talcott Parsons would define as "the Hobbesian problem of order": Weber's definition of *Anstalt*, as an apparatus designed to defend the constituted order, brought "institution" back into a conservative line of thought. For good reason, the Lutheran theologian Rudolph Sohm contrasted it with the liberating force of divine grace, whose purpose is to release Christians' lives from the institutional and juridical cage of the Church. This clash between *officium* and charisma is an early prefiguration of the political–theology polarity that would shape contemporary debate on the institution, splitting it into the two radically opposed fronts that we know so well. On one side there is its defensive, "katechonic" assumption, geared to the necessary maintenance of order; on the other, the messianic option for its destitution. The contrast between institution and movement from which we began finds its beginnings in this dichotomy.

II
The Return

Sociology

The return of institutions onto the twentieth-century cultural scene passed by way of society and not through the state. The nascent discipline of sociology launched a fresh look at institutions before politics and law did, along a line running from Emile Durkheim to Marcel Mauss – bypassing Weber, who remained faithful to the Hobbesian paradigm of order. In an entry written with Paul Fauconnet and published in 1901 in the *Grand Encyclopédie*, Mauss asserts that institutions are the privileged object of sociology.[1] Just as institutions depend on the social context in which they are embedded, the social context is equally shaped by institutions.

This is a first, clear departure from the vertical conception of *institutio*, hierarchically dependent on a superior will. Institutions are not the product of particular wills; they are the product of impersonal forces that precede individuals and determine their behaviors. Rather than forming institutions, individuals are formed by them through their upbringing, transmitted down the chain of generations. This is how French sociology situated itself outside the conceptual framework of legal positivism. The sovereign subject does not shape institutions on the basis of his or her decisions; rather, it is institutions that draw the boundaries within which legislators must move. Individuals do not construct them but discover themselves to have been inscribed from the outset in their grammar.

This prevalence of the objective over the subjective, or of the past over the present, should not be understood as a block that impedes change. On the contrary, the French sociologists insist on the dynamic, indeed, living component of institutional praxis: "True institutions live, that is, change incessantly."[2] This is a turning point from which even the classic theme of *institutio vitae* acquires new meaning: life is not just an object but also a subject of institution, along with which it forms a single movement. The concept undergoes a fresh conversion, which shifts the emphasis from the instituted to the instituent: this is a decisive semantic change with respect to the Weberian-Hobbesian paradigm.

At its center Mauss places the notion of a "total social fact," which not only broadens the language of sociology but integrates it thoroughly into the lexicons of anthropology, psychology, and linguistics. In short, the institution not only becomes the core object of sociological knowledge, but it also forms the locus of mutual exchange between the human sciences. The moment disciplines develop a new epistemological status, they think of themselves as institutional complexes capable of contaminating each other.

But what are the elements that make institutions a channel for diffusing rather than curbing the vital dynamic within society? First and foremost, there is the ability of each institution to generate others in a potentially infinite process. In this regard, Mauss recalls that ancestor worship arises out of funeral rites, exactly as these rites derive from previous magical practices, and so on, in a sort of genealogical regression that tends toward infinity, because each origin appears to issue from a previous one. Just as human life reveals its whole meaning only when plugged into the course of generations, the life of institutions must be situated in a genetic process that extends from the past to the future. Pivotal to this new perspective is its reference to an effectual praxis designed to alter reality. Unlike juridical acts, which are limited to legitimizing settled situations, institutional procedures "are eminently effective; they are creative; they *do* things."[3]

The other distinctive trait of the institution is its concrete, material, bodily character. In a much later essay, titled appropriately "Techniques of the Body," Mauss gives a quick overview of the ways humans have used their bodies over various periods and in different countries: sexual practices, thresholds of excitability, limits of resistance.[4] Each bodily technique is based on nerve and muscle synergies that have a different basis in each social context. There is more, though: by being embodied in different institutions, bodily functions themselves acquire an institutional profile. From the most natural techniques, such as breathing or sleeping, to the most sophisticated, such as the production of fire, human beings have used their bodies technologically, in a way that to some extent recalls a form we spoke about earlier in connection with the Roman institution of nature.

The most powerful point of crossover in the relationship between body and institution, though, is language. It forms the unbreakable bond between individual psyche and social structure and thus the matrix of every other institution. Scholars of linguistics were the first to admit that the phenomena they studied were entirely social, psychological, and physiological at the same time. But even more important in defining the institutional role of language, or the linguistic role of the institution, was the symbolic connection between individual perceptions and collective representations. This is what makes the institution a channel of transit between differential elements in continual circulation rather than an immobile block. The passage from one difference to another ensures that the system of each institution, and that of all of them together, is never saturated, complete, or definitive. According to a formulation picked up by Lévi-Strauss and by Lacanian clinical psychoanalysis,[5] an institution consists of an empty box around which social exchange is determined.

For a specific example, let us recall what Mauss writes about the institution of the gift, practiced by some of the peoples of Polynesia, Melanesia, and the American Northwest. Intertwined in it are religious, legal, economic, political, and aesthetic elements, whose languages are not always distinguishable. What makes these "total phenomena" so fascinating, as far as our inquiry is concerned, is the fact that they reveal instituent praxis at its degree zero, at its initial fusion, in which a rite possesses the value of a law, or a law possesses an economic importance, and so on. While we live in societies that distinguish between persons and things, contracts and gifts, compulsory benefits and gratuitous activities, to the point of making them opposites, the societies studied by Mauss express them freely, in a construct whose contours have become blurred to us.

Law

The first and most influential theorists of legal institutionalism were France's Maurice Hauriou and Italy's Santi Romano. Without entering into detail about their work, we can note that they were the first to go beyond the personalist conception of the medieval *institutio*, later transferred into absolute, earthly sovereignty. Hauriou challenges the positivist doctrine – backed in Germany by legal theorists Carl Gerber, Paul Laband, and Georg Jellinek – that interprets the rules of law as an expression of state will. To argue that everything the law produces emanates from the legislator's will means to lose sight of the long formation process that nation-states themselves undergo, along with the laws and customs that precede and, at times, surpass them.

But Hauriou also criticizes the opposing theory, voiced above all by Léon Duguit: in the wake of Durkheim, Duguit reduces juridical forms to the objective expression of social processes, causing them to lose all autonomy. Against both these tendencies, voluntaristic on the one hand and deterministic on the other, the new current gives juridical importance to a series of institutions that do not coincide with the state institution, while maintaining their distinctiveness from society. In Hauriou's theory, the institution generated by a given social environment may or may not be embodied in a legal person, resulting in two types: person-institutions, such as states, political parties, and unions; and thing-institutions, independent from the state structure.[6] Although Hauriou focuses particularly on the first type, his mention of objective entities, namely, those that are not embodied in a legal subject, already transports the theory of institution outside the old personalist vocabulary. This is an important shift toward an expanded and diversified concept of institutional praxis. In it, Hauriou mixes cultural elements with different provenances, both spiritual and biological at the same time, as diverse as the authors from whom he takes inspiration, ranging from Gabriel Tarde to Henri Bergson and Claude Bernard. Because of this conceptual ubiquity, however, although Hauriou contests the centrality of the state in favor of an institutional pluralism, he never entirely abandons it.

This basic uncertainty is precisely what Italian jurist Santi Romano critically examines: during the same years, he developed the most technically rigorous and theoretically radical theory of institutionalism. The leading exponent of Vittorio Emanuele Orlando's historical school of law, he occupied high-level government posts, including during the Fascist regime, without this negatively affecting his theoretical rigor. He criticizes his French colleague for "being carried away with the idea of modeling his institutions on the broadest among them, that is, the state."[7] This is the same state, moreover, whose crisis Romano had declared in a famous 1909 lecture at the University of Pisa.[8] That speech, which proved to be prescient regarding what was about to happen in Europe, can be seen as the true birth of legal institutionalism. Reacting to the self-celebratory narrative of the modern state, which makes it the sole bearer of public law, Romano enlarges its boundaries to include a multiplicity of non-state institutions. In his masterpiece on the legal order, he reverses the relationship between state and law: while the idea of "law" is independent from that of "state," it is impossible to define the state without falling back on the concept of law.

In this outspoken defense of the juridical domain with respect to the political, economic, and sociological spheres, one recognizes a conservative element – easily explainable, after all, in someone who worked in close contact with the Fascist regime – but also an original way of conceiving of the whole world from the legal perspective. No discipline – economics, sociology, or political science – has the performative power of the law, to which Romano assigns a peculiar vitality, represented specifically by the institution. Every system – of any kind – is an institution, and vice versa. Only this horizontal expansion of the legal system appears able to keep pace with the complexity of contemporary society. Where else did the state's crisis sprout from if not its inability to open itself to the demands of new collective subjects – groups, associations, organizations – expressed by a society that can no longer be contained within the narrow confines of state sovereignty?

But Romano does not restrict himself to challenging the exclusivity of sovereign power by articulating it within the plurality of systems: he deconstructs the very category of legal person as the sole source of "law." The source of law is not only the legislator's will but also the need expressed by society: a power capable of acting not only *extra legem* (outside the law) but also *contra legem* (against the law), forcing legislators to repeal laws already put into force or to create new ones. On these lines, Romano makes the law a creative force capable of producing new legal realities.

This expands the confines of "order" (*ordinamento*) exponentially, extending it to all organized social forces – those inside, outside, or even opposed to the state, such as illegal associations or revolutionary movements aimed at overthrowing it. The state may view them as hostile powers and combat them as such, but the fact remains that, in themselves, they are perfectly legal, for the sole reason that they have an internal organization. Denial of this, continues Romano, brushing against the outermost limits of his ontology, stems purely from an ethical judgment, which, as such, lies outside the law's horizon. And he adds a surprising argument for someone who worked as a jurist under the Fascist regime: a revolutionary association that aims to overturn an unjust state order would be more ethical than the same state that declares it illegal.

Going even further in his critique of state sovereignty, in another, more extreme version of institutionalism that also breaks the relationship between order and organization, is the Russian-born French sociologist of law Georges Gurvitch. Distinguishing between an organized and an unorganized law, Gurvitch assigns more energy to the latter than to the former. Unorganized law can exist without organized law, but the reverse does not hold true. On the contrary, if organized law shuts itself inside its normative armor, then law turns into a form of domination destined to oppress society. In this radical version of institutionalism, the law not only arises from the bottom of a society riddled by tensions and conflicts but is also fully immanent to it. Law does not depend on a transcendental sovereign: it is an integral part of demands and movements that are irreducible to the established codes and laws.

Philosophy

The third type of critical engagement with the concept of institution, distinct from but contiguous with sociology and law, is the path opened by philosophy. To understand its beginnings, one must look primarily at the phenomenological current, started in Germany by the studies of Edmund Husserl and disseminated in France by Maurice Merleau-Ponty beginning in the 1950s. But why phenomenology in particular – a thought that appears to be quite remote from any political projection? In reality, this formulaic image of phenomenology is contradicted by the ethical and political engagement demonstrated by several of its exponents. It could be argued, on the other hand, that in other respects phenomenology's apparently impolitical positioning protected it against some of the choices of political philosophy that later proved to be unsuccessful or highly problematic.

Looking at France, the perspectives of philosophers such as Raymond Aron and Jean-Paul Sartre, widely influential in liberal and Marxist circles, are difficult to associate with an innovative idea of instituent praxis. As for Germany, no institutionalist turn could be attributed to the post-Hegelian culture, anchored to a monistic philosophy of the state, or to the Heideggerian ontology, which, after its deplorable involvement with Nazism, was forced to retreat in an impolitical direction. Within this framework, in short, phenomenology remained the only major philosophical strand that spoke the language of institution, along two different and complementary axes. The first is the relationship between subject and object; the other, the concept of "relationship," which puts the individual subject in a web of shared reciprocity with others. Nevertheless, both these conceptual moves, initiated by Husserl, remain incomplete, since the subject's consciousness remains central to its conception. This is the shortcoming to which Merleau-Ponty responded, by nudging phenomenological semantics in a more intensely historical and political direction. The turn he imparts to the phenomenological paradigm consists in a shift from a philosophy of consciousness to a thought of living corporeality, liberating its historical and political significance.[9]

At the core of this shift is the nexus between the vertical dimension of historicity and the horizontal one of relationship. Relationship with otherness can develop only in a framework that reconstructs a connection between past and future. This means introducing novelty, inherent in human activity, into a succession that maintains contact with its roots. For this reason, Merleau-Ponty introduces a clear difference between the concepts of "instituent praxis" and "constituent power," a distinction generally used by theorists of revolution. Whereas constituent power, in both its right- and left-wing versions, reproduces the theological concept of *creatio ex nihilo* but on a secular level, instituent praxis affirms a processual quality that embeds the new inside an already instituted world.[10]

This is a significant difference, both political and philosophical in nature. Just as every "assumption" is a "resumption" of something coming before it, the latter projects itself forward, altering the next event – even radically. Far from being absolute, the instituent creation is conditioned by a series of constraints that channel its action into a set of already constructed tracks. But "conditioned" does not signify "determined," because the new meaning cannot be entirely explained by the pre-existing one. A possible point of juncture between the mediated reality of the instituted moment and the unmediated reality of the instituent moment is the concept of "emergence." Something emerges from something else, without being determined by it, and transforms it; as happened, for example, to Freudian psychoanalysis in relation to the psychological science of its time.

But, in addition to altering the object that it institutes, instituent praxis also transforms its own subject – the subjects that put it into action. Instead of assuming subjectivity as a given, however, placed before and outside what it produces from one time to the next, instituent thought views subjectivity as issuing from its own praxis. It appeals to a "process of subjectification" rather than to specific subjects. Simply put, the action of instituting produces the same subjectivity that puts it into action. By instituting something new, individuals institute themselves, transforming themselves with respect to their initial mode of being. While a constituent power always presupposes a subject that is already formed – a sovereign people, a Jacobin party, or even a revolutionary multitude – instituent thought views subjectivity as arising out of the same institutional mechanisms in which it participates.

This is what makes it possible to speak of an impersonal subject, which breaks down, from another side, the coupling between institution and personhood established by constitutional law. The reference to the impersonal stems from the critique of the legal person as the sole bearer of institution, specifically that of the person of the state. By definition, the instituent process can never be identified with a single person, placed before and above its dynamic; but neither can it be limited to an encounter, or dialogue, between two persons or parties undergoing legal action. An institution always envisages a third party to ensure a general interest, mediating any potential conflict between particular interests. It always has an impersonal membrane between the two, which filters the immediacy of the face-to-face encounter and prevents it from degenerating into a violent clash. In this sense, it contains something of what Hegel called "objective spirit": a point of view that situates subjective interests, or desires, on a wider horizon, giving them an objective character.

Politics

In the revival of institutional thought, politics is a key player, of course, alongside sociology, law, and philosophy. Situated at the point of connection and tension with society, it occupies a high-profile place in this renewed interest. The author who most aids us in understanding this triangulation is Claude Lefort, a favorite student of Merleau-Ponty and editor of his works. For Lefort, the task of politics is specifically "the institution of the social."[11] To understand the meaning of this expression, we should not confuse "institution" with any institutions already present in society; rather, it refers to political praxis itself, which is instituent per se.

Institutions, societies, and politics are connected by the function of conflict. Indeed, politics institutes society by dividing it into two inevitably conflicting camps; or, rather, by making it aware of the division that traverses it from the very beginning. Society – every society, past and present – is always divided between opposing values and interests. But often it does not know this, imagining itself united in the ostensible cohesiveness of the people. Instituent praxis makes society aware that it is divided and conscious of the precise place where the division occurs. This explains the complex relationship that connects politics and society: although they are not identical, one could not exist without the other. Society is the only space in which politics is practiced; but the reverse is also true. Just as politics could not exist without society, society cannot exist without politics, because without the qualifying function of politics, without the decisions that it makes over time, every society would be the same as all others. Only politics – and to be more exact, the conflict that courses through it – gives a society its specific meaning, differentiating it from all others. For example, it is the political institution of the Ancien Régime that distinguishes it from the modern one, or a democratic society from a totalitarian one.

What separates them specifically is the role and position of power, but also the quality of the conflict out of which power originates. In a totalitarian society the space of power is filled once and for all by a single party and its leader; in a democratic society the space of power is an empty placeholder, so to speak, which can therefore be contested and occupied from one time to the next, but always temporarily, by the party that prevails in the political confrontation. Nevertheless, just because its place is vacant does not mean that power does not exist or that it should be eliminated. Even in democratic societies, it exercises an irreplaceable function: that of instituting them as such.[12]

This point needs to be clarified vis-à-vis anarchic suggestions currently resurfacing from several quarters of contemporary philosophy.[13] There is no such thing as a society without power, nor has there ever been. This is so intuitively evident that it does not need to be proven. But in democratic regimes, power is anything but external to the social dynamic, imposed and dropped in from on high: power is its very expression, in the sense that it is the temporary outcome of the confrontation – the clash – between the interests and values represented by the social parts. Power shapes society, in its turn, by demarcating the way the latter operates or distributes its resources but, above all, the symbolic form it takes.

In short, from the instituent point of view, "power" should not be understood as a *dispositif* of domination but as that which provides every society with its institutional configuration. Obviously, the role, form, and prerogatives of power vary historically according to different social organizations. In absolute states it is concentrated in a single point – situated at the tip of the social body, in its head; in democratic societies it is spread out among its various parts. Even more important to note, however, is that while in authoritarian societies power tends to neutralize conflict, in democratic ones, power is a function of conflict. Indeed, institutions are the places, procedures, and practices within which power and conflict relate. Institution is what ensures that political conflict will continue to play its active, regulatory role in society.

From this point of view, speaking in genealogical terms, the first thinker of instituent power was Machiavelli.[14] No one grasped and theorized the productive character of political conflict in society the way he did: not in opposition to order but in a necessary relationship with it.[15] Unlike Hobbes, who puts order and conflict in alternation, making the former's birth dependent on the latter's extinction, for Machiavelli conflict is the fundamental engine of political order. He is perhaps the only modern thinker for whom conflict is both primordial and insuperable. Conflict is primordial, that is, instituent, because it is not preceded by anything – not even by the parties in conflict with each other, who, rather than being its cause, are its effect. It is insuperable because it is connected constitutively to political activity.

For this reason, Machiavelli's political ontology, unlike Aristotle's, is literally unfounded: in part, because it is exposed to absolute contingency, which blocks it from any teleological temptation, but also because there is no single foundation at the base of society – let alone the foundation of the One – but rather a binary *dispositif* that cannot be reduced to unity. From the outset, the social has been divided, and division has always been social. Consequently, if kept within the confines of politics, antagonism is not destructive to sociability. Quite the opposite: antagonism is the most intrinsic expression of sociability; it is the form that coexistence takes. Only through conflict can society relate to itself and recognize itself as a society, both one and binary at the same time. Therefore, society cannot be the result of a contract between individuals who choose to leave the conflictual state of nature to enter the social state. First, because, since society is primordial, there is no prior state of nature; and, secondly, because the social state, which, as we have said, in no way excludes conflict, is instituted by it. Hence, conflict is not only primordial but also inextinguishable.

To sum up, institution is what holds opposing interests together, thereby preventing conflict from degenerating into violence. To stay with Machiavelli, consider for example the Roman institute of the tribune of the plebs, discussed throughout his *Discourses on Livy*. Arising out of political conflict between the patriciate and the plebs, it had the role of organizing conflict vis-à-vis the various power relations as they arose. Thus, unlike Hobbes, who connects politics with the state, Machiavelli ties it to the dynamics of institutions. For Hobbes, the only institution possible and necessary for the survival of society is that of the state. For Machiavelli, who lived in sixteenth-century Italy – which had no state – political, civil, religious, and military institutions extend beyond the state horizon, both preceding and surpassing it.

Certainly, it is not easy to grasp the instituent connection between unity and division, order and conflict, that Machiavelli recognized at the dawn of modern politics. At the heart of the instituent paradigm there remains the enigma of an antagonism internal to order, acting as its driving force rather than opposing it. How can a society be unified by its own division? And how can competition produce order without sliding into absolute antagonism? To answer these questions, we need to recognize the role of the negative in instituent praxis. This is what we will do in the next chapter.

III
The Productivity of the Negative

The End of Mediation

Institution has an essential relationship with the concept of "negation," which explains the difficulty theorists have in recognizing the full potential of its meaning. This negativity does not pertain to the effects of the instituent act but to its very nature. It arises out of the coexistence of two different, even opposite, semantic lines in the word that refer respectively to stasis and movement. A first polarity is already apparent in the distinction between the noun form, *institution*, and the verb form, *to institute*. But this distinction does not suffice to resolve an ambivalence that recurs, to a different degree, in both the noun and the verb. Both terms, derived from the Latin compound *in-statuere*, contain two colliding tones that are prone to negate each other, although without ever canceling each other out entirely. Indeed, institution's peculiar character may be said to reside precisely in their mutual implication.

———

Such a character alludes to the act of foundation or establishment of something new that did not exist. To institute means to establish something that was previously non-existent. From this point of view, instituent praxis indicates a beginning that changes the previous framework, even radically, by introducing a novelty into it. But, at the same time, the instituted novelty is a "state" more than a becoming, an entity destined to "stay," by resisting disintegration. For this reason, paradoxically, a movement that is instituent tends to negate itself, that is, to create immobility. It elevates, raises, erects something that must be kept standing, remain firmly planted on its own base.

This is the source of the concept's paradox, which seems to put it at odds with itself: the result of the instituent movement is the stability of the institution. Rather than eradicate ancient roots, novelty becomes incorporated into them, at once extending and strengthening them. This is the source of the singular character of its logic, which holds together movement and stability, change and permanence, innovation and preservation. Institution is not born *ex nihilo*; it always arises out of something that was also instituted in its time, something to be simultaneously preserved and innovated. But – and this is the question that continues to challenge thinkers, without receiving a convincing answer – how can we preserve a novelty without negating it?

The problem of the negative returns. For the instituent process to be productive, it must give life to something that does not preexist it. And, indeed, once instituted, the institution acquires a reality external to the movement that produced it. This exteriority or autonomy of the result with respect to the subjective intention that led to it appears impossible to eliminate. It is what Hegel called "objective spirit." This is the moment when spirit is realized in the objective effectuality of institutions, at whose apex stands the supreme institution: the state. This conception is predicated on the impossibility of the subject's activity enduring without becoming objectified into something that somehow surpasses it.

Institution expresses this intrinsically contradictory implication of freedom and necessity, subject and object, inside and outside – in more general terms, positive and negative. Hegel's thought is the dialectical apex of this contradiction in a historical phase when a possible point of mediation between movement and institution, innovation and stability, still seemed possible. The objectification of what he defines as "spirit," that is, the very movement of the real, is not yet estrangement: it is a process of realization through the negative. The tension between freedom and necessity is still capable of containing the opposites without exploding. The political state is not perceived as oppression but as the expression of civil society.

This interpretive framework would shatter only a few decades later. With Marx, the philosophy of mediation had already been overturned into a theory of revolution, while Nietzsche views the Hegelian ethical state as the "cold monster" that governs our lives. The "iron cage" that Max Weber speaks about in his turn merely translates into more urbane terms a distrust toward institutions that have become frozen in a soulless objectivity. The possibility of thinking about the negative as a dialectical power that can include the positive, a possibility still present in Hegel, now vanishes. After him, affirmation and negation separate radically into their own orbits, armed and moving against each other. Institutional thought succumbs to the same fate of laceration. The coexistence of innovation and preservation, intrinsic to the concept, shatters in the frontal collision between institutions and movements with which we began. All twentieth-century political philosophy tends to split into either-or polarities incapable of dialoguing with each other. Institutional rigidification and the rejection of institutions become two dead-end streets that lead the issue into an impasse.

At the heart of this standoff is an inability to conceive of the negative in a productive way – to deliver it from contemporary philosophy's tendency of either absolutizing or repressing it. On one side, along a line originating with Heidegger, the negative is absolutized to the point of severing any relationship between being (*das Sein*) and beings (*die Seienden*), in what is defined as "the ontological difference"; on the other, Henri Bergson cancels out the negative in the name of an equally exclusionary affirmation. What is lost, however, is the capacity to conceive of the negative affirmatively, something crucial for instituent thought.[1]

This is what Paul Ricoeur observes critically in an article on the institution.[2] Its main message is a positive reformulation of what anti-institutionalists stigmatize in terms of "alienation." Dialogue and exchange between people can only take place against an institutional backdrop whose purpose is to prevent "face-to-face" relations from degenerating into confrontations. To avoid the internalization of relations exploding into a conflict without quarter, they must necessarily pass through a moment of externalization that in some way objectivizes the terms of the confrontation. Instituent praxis is situated precisely on this fluctuating border between inside and outside, identity and alterity, order and conflict. Contrary to the utopia of "reconciliation at any cost," institution not only recognizes that conflict is irreconcilable but also prevents absolute pacificism from flipping into terrorism, passing from unconditional love to the vigilante justice of the people's courts, as it did during the Terror of the French Revolution.[3] The point (obscured by all political theologies, both reactionary and revolutionary) is that only our relationship with the negative saves us from the dream – or nightmare – of unconditional affirmativeness. But to understand this we need to go beyond a unilaterally negative idea of the institution.

Hence the need for a paradigmatic shift: if institutions continue to appear as a cohesive block of power and repression, all that remains is the messianic option of their destitution. Nothing is more ineffective and simultaneously dangerous as the neoanarchist myth of a society simplified into a stark alternative between repressive institutions or no institutions. The most recent form of this myth is today's growing demand for direct democracy in opposition to the institutions of representative democracy. The debate on institutions slides toward two extreme, irreconcilable poles: on one end, progressive institutional sclerosis; on the other, freedom from institutions. The road we need to take passes instead via a new juncture between institutions and freedom.

Institution

Humanity's Prosthesis

We have seen that institutional logic expresses a fundamental contradiction: it binds together freedom and necessity, subject and object, inside and outside. The coupled terms cannot separate or overlap without disrupting the equilibrium of their relationship. All institutional thought moves within this tension, in the awareness that the contradiction can never be resolved. Obviously, this thought follows different pathways, different interpretive axes, depending on the role assigned to each pole and to the line that holds them in relation. Should this line be understood as a limit that divides, or as an edge that joins together? Is it a separating barrier, or a pivot around which institutional praxis rotates? In short, is the negative inherent in institution something that condemns it to repetition, or the driving force that enables it to transform?

Similar questions could be asked about the relationship between nature and *techne*. At issue is whether they lie at the ends of a single segment or on parallel planes destined never to meet. Do human needs occur naturally, or do they require institutional filters that allow them to be satisfied? These questions form the core of a discipline that, primarily in Germany, has assumed the name of "philosophical anthropology," whose best-known exponent is Arnold Gehlen.

Like other institutional theorists, Gehlen is distinguished by the way he handles the negative. He certainly does not undervalue its presence; in fact, he makes it the premise of his anthropology. Drawing on Nietzsche's idea of humans as "*the still undetermined animals (das noch nicht festgestellte Tier)*,"[4] Gehlen ties human fragility to a lack of natural instincts. This deficiency, which places humans in a condition of initial inferiority with respect to other animals, requires them to equip themselves with artificial tools, which ultimately lead to institutions. The inadequacy of humans' natural tools denies them the immediate gratification of their primary needs, so they substitute technological prostheses to enable them to bridge the gap separating them from the animal world that originally dominated them.

This process can be explained both in phylogenetic and ontogenetic terms. Either way, it is anything but linear. On the contrary, the process passes through a series of stops and detours that create continuous filters between the goal sought and the means used to obtain it. The first of these is the substitution of the natural with the artificial. Like Hobbes, Gehlen believes that we can only pass into a civil state by first renouncing a state of nature; he thus places a hiatus between vital needs and the actions required to satisfy them. To overcome its initial inferiority and facilitate its self-preservation, the human lifeform compartmentalizes its impulses and selects them according to their function. The second form of stabilization for humans in a potentially hostile environment is the use of representations to reduce environmental complexity, thereby containing its indeterminacy. The third and most conspicuous form of immunization put into action by the human animal to combat its original incompleteness is "exoneration" (*Entlastung*). Only by relieving themselves of burdens, restrictions, or impediments – by removing themselves from the flood of impulses that stimulate them – can humans funnel their experience into a meaningful channel.

45

Without the intervention of institutions, though, located outside them like a set of prostheses needed to replace missing limbs, these steps would be insufficient to ensure their survival. In institutions, human actions translated into norms are crystallized into an objective order that subjects perceive as already in force the instant they enter into relationship with it. Although institutions only come into play at the end of the hominization process, they appear to be its preconditions, guiding it in specific directions. The function of institutions is to free humans from the task of organizing their life in a burdensome environment, by restraining life inside pre-established boundaries. Thus, freed from the pressure of the "here and now," they can plan for a future time; no longer limited to just living, they can commit themselves to leading their lives.[5]

This should not be understood as limitless progress. On the contrary, the underlying tone of this philosophical anthropology is strongly tinged with an anti-Enlightenment bias. If humans were left to their own resources, without the protection of institutional canopies external to them, they would not be able to withstand the many drives that surge up internally or the environmental pressure that weighs down on them externally. From this point of view, Gehlen's critique of Rousseau's naturalism is just as pointed as his criticism of Hegel's idealism. The difficulty in understanding the vital role of institutions stems from the incurably idealistic character of modern philosophy. Without stable containers capable of preserving ideas – such as institutions – they would never survive their constant dizzying flow and exchange. We would need to set up institutional husks just to ensure that they last long enough, much less to preserve their content.

Something similar must be said about legal formulas, which require stable structures within which to take material form – law offices, courtrooms, administrative systems, parliamentary commissions; not to mention religion, kept alive by ecclesiastical organizations that give institutional body to formulations and teachings that would otherwise be destined to disperse. As just one of the many prophetic messages crowding the ancient world, how long would Christianity have lasted without the formidable legal machine of a church to defend it and propagate its doctrine through time? All this laborious social engineering is threatened today by a "dismantling of institutions,"[6] produced by the selfsame technological progress that birthed them, and that now, along with its vertiginous development, threatens to sweep them away.

The explicitly conservative tone of Gehlen's discourse is unmistakable – not surprising, given the blatant political compromises he made with the Nazi regime. What is missing from his theory of institutions, and from his negative anthropology in general, is an adequate assessment of the original sociability and, therefore, creativity of human nature. His theory runs the risk of flipping over into a renaturalization of the selfsame institutions that spurred humankind beyond the natural world. This is what Adorno objects to in a well-known discussion with Gehlen:[7] institutions are not just a technical prosthesis originating from the deficiency of human nature; they are the product of a particular historical development. Therefore, our fate does not depend solely on the solidity of institutions but, above all, on their capacity to change.

Institution

Instincts and Institutions

In a short text from the 1950s, starting from assumptions not that distant from Gehlen's, Gilles Deleuze interprets the negative of instituent praxis in a more open key. Unlike those who see in institutions a coercion of vital forces, he recognizes an affirmative power aimed at promoting their development. Institutions do not suffocate the free unfurling of instincts, and, under certain conditions, they even allow them to expand. Instead of inhibiting natural tendencies, institutions open up spaces for their gratification that would otherwise be precluded.

He arrives at this conclusion by disconnecting institution and law, shifting the latter onto the side of the negative and reserving a positive connotation for the former. Whereas laws enclose human action inside boundaries marked by obligations and prohibitions, institutions provide functional models to facilitate its realization. This allows Deleuze to argue his unusual thesis that, "tyranny is a regime in which there are many laws and few institutions; democracy is a regime in which there are many institutions, and few laws."[8] Underpinning this assertion is a reversal of priorities in the relationship between law, politics, and society. Legal norms and political decision-making do not precede historically instituted needs; rather, they follow them. Therefore, the true legislator is not the person who legislates, and much less the person who commands: it is the person who institutes. Out of this comes a shift destined to retie the knot between the state of nature and the political state that Hobbes had severed so drastically at the dawn of modern political philosophy.

The starting point for this line of reasoning, which gives a new value to human nature, is not Rousseau, however, but Hume. There are two reasons for this. First, because through Hume's utilitarianism Deleuze places himself outside the mythology of the social contract; and, secondly, because instead of opposing nature to culture, he integrates them in a way that abandons modern dualism and embraces a new perspective. In utilitarianism, the backbone of society is institution, not law. While the aim of a society governed by law is to guarantee its subjects or citizens the enjoyment of natural rights, legitimized by the social contract, the intention of a society shaped by institutions is to form citizens into subjects of a praxis adapted to their needs. This creates a 180-degree rotation in the relationship between law, politics, and society. In contrast to the Hobbesian model, which places the political and the juridical before the social, the utilitarian model starts from society, adapting politics and law to it. Instead of preceding social needs, political decision-making and legal rules derive from them. In this arrangement, the institution of life springs up from within its natural stratum rather than contradicting it. Even Deleuze's reference to jurisprudence, which he opposes to the "force of law," offers a plastic, creative version of law that never clashes with social demands but rather develops in a working relationship with them.

This does not lead Deleuze to eliminate the negative, though, at least not in this phase of his philosophical journey. Expelled from the social, the negative resurfaces in instituent praxis. Although the institution remains in contact with the nature out of which it arises, it does fully identify with it. The edge that joins institution and

nature together also separates them. Unlike philosophical anthropology, Deleuze does not view institutions as
a substitute for deficient instincts: institutions complete
instincts, making them effectual, as it were. What was a
conflict or an alternative in Gehlen's thought becomes a
shared existence in Deleuze's.

But institution and nature are not connected by
equivalence or superimposition. However rooted in
nature, the artifice of institution is not identical to it.
It is one thing to say that natural drives are gratified
through institutional means, quite another to say that
they are the same thing. Between one and the other
there remains a membrane that, no matter how thin,
continues to separate them. It is true that institutional
intervention is required to satisfy natural tendencies;
for example, sexual needs are gratified in the institution
of marriage, just as greed is gratified in the institution
of property. But marriage and property lie beyond the
instincts to which they respond, preserving a core that
transcends them. The transition from nature to culture
remains perpetually open; but it is neither immediate
nor linear, because it demands a deviation implicit in
the tool through which it is carried out. If the result is
propulsive, because it expands the natural tendency,
the means used to arrive at this end also act to curb the
impulse.

If this were not the case – if the institution remained
within the bounds of the natural tendency – the transition from nature to culture would always follow the
same route, as it does for animal instincts, all of which
are satisfied in the same way. Not so for humans, who
are differentiated by the type of artifice they employ
on each occasion. No matter where birds are located,

they always build their nests in the same way, whereas humans in different places and times build their homes differently depending on their preferences. However necessary to nature, institutions are always different, because they vary according to the mindset, customs, and, above all, the imagination of their inventors. Before institutions are set up, they are imagined.

This is where the unique character of individuals resides in contrast to the biological species to which they belong. The individuality of a human being is never flattened into the uniformity of instinct: unlike that of animals, human instinct is not perfect, but it is perfectible, because it is mediated by language and intelligence. There is always a third element standing between individual and species, constituted by society. Its presence reveals the institution's dual character: at once natural and historical, necessary and contingent, spontaneous and obligatory. True, the repetition of circumstances – such as sleeping at night or eating during the day – produces a chain of recurrences that makes the future predictable; but only partially, since an individual can always decide to sleep during the day or eat at night.

No matter how necessary the institution is to satisfying basic needs, it is not instinct. It requires a distance that – if it does not negate instinct directly, as does the law – splits it in two, through the membrane of the imagination. This reverses the proportions between institution and law. It might be said that an institution is an affirmation of a negative, in contrast to the law, which is a negation of a positive. What puts them in opposition is not an absolute choice between affirmation and negation but the way they intersect and the perspectival point from which this intersection is viewed. The law looks at the positive – at natural givens and tendencies – from the point of view of negation, while the institution looks at the negative from the point of view of affirmation.

The Social Imaginary

The relationship between institution and imagination is crucial to the theory of another author, Cornelius Castoriadis,[9] certainly the most radical in asserting the creative character of instituent praxis. This creativity stems on the one hand from the virtually identical definition of the two terms: to imagine something means to institute it, to make a non-being into a being; and on the other hand, from the precedence of this instituent imaginary over every other sphere of reality. If the real, in all its forms and manifestations, is always instituted, then nothing exists before the act that gives it expression – neither individual nor society, nature or culture, economy or politics.

In this respect, Castoriadis's theory lies outside all the major philosophical and political currents of the twentieth century. It stands apart from liberalism, which puts the individual first, but it is equally aloof from Marxism, which makes the institution a result of the mode of production. Instead, for Castoriadis, both the individual and the mode of production acquire meaning only if they are socially instituted. An individual is always inscribed within social relations that condition his or her behavior, just as a class gains institutional importance in the relationship it establishes with associations, unions, and parties.

Castoriadis's instituent imaginary stands equally

remote, however, from philosophies that view the imagination as merely the subject's simple representation of an object, whether truthful or deceptive. He believes instead that the imaginary activity is what institutes both subject and object, in addition to their relationship. Subject and object exist only in their mutual implication within an already instituted context. This does not mean that the social imaginary creates being from nothingness, within a completely empty field. If this were the case, it would mean that there exists an original condition in which, at a certain moment, the spark of institution ignites. This is what Christian theology intends by "genesis" and modern political philosophy by "social contract," according to a narrative that opposes a state of nature to a political state. Instead, as the Roman jurists understood, there is no such thing as a nature that has not been juridically instituted.

This explains the distance Castoriadis takes from Gehlen's philosophical anthropology. The institution is not an artificial prosthesis that compensates for a deficient natural endowment, providing human behaviors with preformed structures within which to be channeled. This sort of reasoning is tantamount to superimposing an equally ahistorical, deterministic outcome on an initial naturalism: starting from some deficient conception of human nature, one deduces the need to subject it to artificial devices that drastically reduce human freedom of choice. Castoriadis reverses this thought process: since human nature is instituted from the beginning, institutions contain a natural core from which we do not need to escape but, rather, develop according to the choices we make over time. But this decision-making can never be abstracted from the context in which it takes place. Institutions take form only from what is already instituted.

Of course, this works the other way around too, even more so, preventing institutions from becoming rigidified into lifeless fixities. No institution is completely autonomous from the energy that brought it into being, continuously transforming it. While every human praxis tends naturally to become institutionalized, every institution is altered by the insurgence of a new praxis that mobilizes it incessantly. This fact is especially important in regard to theories of desistence popular today, given that desistence, too, if imagined as such, is also instituted. Humans can and, indeed, will inevitably modify history with their behaviors, but they cannot escape it. Therefore, despite all the many announcements, history has neither an ending nor an end, whatever meaning one wishes to attach to these words.

But history does not have a beginning either. Although scored by countless origins – every time something rises up or someone comes into the world – history has no origin. If it did, this origin would precede the process, thereby transcending it. But if that were the case, we would fall into a form of disguised theology that in political theory has often taken the name of "constituent power." All theories of constituent power, whether formulated by the right or left, have always ended up sacrificing the instituted to the instituent, knocking history off its hinges before being disrupted by it in their turn.

To protect ourselves from this eventuality, we must keep alive the subtle balance between being and becoming, history and nature, that gives instituent praxis a dialectical form. Human activity cannot endure in the absence of a negative capable of creating friction in the flow of becoming. It needs to settle and stabilize itself in ritual, symbolic, social, and political practices, without which it would be incapable of withstanding the pressure of time – but without slipping into a form of naturalistic determinism, because no human nature exists outside the historical and social *dispositifs* that shape it at various times, in different ways and with differing results.

The ultimate outcome of this process is when the imaginary assumes a specifically political form, coinciding with the transition from heteronomy to autonomy. This is the moment when a given society recognizes itself as free from transcendent constraints, whether theological or natural, and relies on self-determination. Politics is the self-reflective capacity through which society overcomes its alienation to external powers and recognizes itself as the master of its own destiny. Only then can it be said that a society fully assumes its own historicity.

IV
Beyond the State

Sovereignless Institutions

Rediscovering Institutions is the title of a book by James G. March and Johan P. Olsen.[1] Published in 1989, it marks a symbolic watershed with respect to the preceding 30 years, a period characterized, on the one hand, by a devaluing of institutional logic and, on the other, its rejection. As already noted, although opposed, methodological individualism and Marxist culture have found themselves allies in this work of deinstitutionalizing politics. Instead of being vital players in the political game, institutions have long been considered mere containers of individual and collective behaviors. Social classes, economic models, and technological transformations have appeared as determining factors in political dynamics to a much greater extent than instituent praxis. Then, at a certain moment, the scene changed: institutions began to appear increasingly important in defining, guiding, and transforming political agendas. And political agendas, in their turn, had to give greater consideration to institutions, whose importance received such intense recognition that it led to talk of a "new discovery."

Nevertheless, unlike what March and Olsen believe, this "rediscovery" of institutions did not issue from what Gabriel Almond defined as a "return to the state" but, on the contrary, from an increasingly blatant diminishment of its importance.[2] It is true that the state has always been interpreted, not without grounds, as the first and most comprehensive institution. And yet this very primacy, in some ways taken for granted, has been undermined by globalization processes that intensified in the late 1980s, consequent to the ending of the Cold War. Today we know that those processes were contradictory and inequitable, challenged, often successfully, by opposing tendencies and resistance movements. But, over the long run, it is highly doubtful that anything will be able to stop, much less reverse, the decline of the Westphalian model, namely, the modern order based on the full autonomy of sovereign states as the sole holder of political decision-making power.

New institutionalism, without envisaging an entirely improbable return to premodern or even neomedieval conditions, has been unleashed overall by the crisis of the sovereign regime, which has long been replaced, or at least splintered, by governmental practices to which it cannot be reduced. Of course, nothing can be excluded in the future. The clash with Islamic fundamentalism has already struck at and definitively buried globalization's *belle époque*, along with its related "end of history" ideology. Nor can we exclude a prolonged conflict between China and the West, which is already divided internally between its Atlantic and European interests. But in this case, too, the conflict is limited for now to the economic terrain, inside a world unified by global finance and information technology.

Even what is defined improperly as "sovereignism" appears to be a form of resistance to ongoing processes rather than something capable of intercepting the future. The geopolitical situation is certainly evolving very quickly. In the short run, the terrible pandemic-related crisis may very well create forms of phobic closure within national borders. But the very possibility of countering the virus with structural measures, in medical and economic terms, nevertheless requires a network of connections on a global or at least continental scale.

The role of institutions in this dynamic appears critical in several ways, provided that they are not limited to consolidating existing powers: they must be able to manage transformations as they occur, making themselves the primary channel for changes. This can only happen if, instead of trying uselessly to protect themselves from social conflicts, they give voice to the conflicts that the crisis has exacerbated, in an unbreakable connection with the discourses of economy and law. The function of institutions has long been recognized in these two areas. As far as economics is concerned, this importance has also been demonstrated at a symbolic level by the awarding of the Nobel Prize to institutionalist economists James M. Buchanan in 1986, Ronald H. Coase in 1991, and Douglass C. North in 1993. Central to their work is a focus on the rules that simultaneously guide and constrain the decisions of economic actors.

Here, too, there is a clear inversion of the neoclassical economic approach, which undervalued the role of institutions compared to the criterion of rationality adopted. It assumed that markets tend toward efficiency, regardless of the contextual situation. Pushing back against this obviously optimistic idea, institutionalist economists instead identify uncertainty as the predominant feature of markets. Institutions are the only instrument for keeping this uncertainty under control. The institutional paradigm is therefore once again considered a fundamental tool for both understanding economics and reorienting its aims. Of course, not all institutions are equal in their effects. Indeed, in *Institutions, Institutional Change and Economic Performance*, North distinguishes between institutions that inhibit economic development and others that encourage it.[3] In general, the former make contractual practices murky, thereby predetermining outcomes and concealing information; the latter make rules transparent and markets competitive.

This reference to the rules calls into question the function of the law, located at the heart of the institutionalist paradigm. From a certain point of view, the law is the source of all institutions – even non-juridical ones – which necessarily use a normative language. But, here too, rather than attesting to the juridicity of institutions, it signals their progressive emancipation from the sovereign yoke. Today we are witnessing a true proliferation of legal institutions that are independent from national systems, located at sub-, supra-, or transnational levels. In an increasing number of sectors – from commerce to healthcare, technology, and communications – national regulations are expanded or overstepped by conventions that make the law into a shifting, continuously changing mosaic. Ever since nations lost their exclusive right to legislate, new actors are gaining access to the creation of rules and regulations, giving rise to legal procedures that run transversally rather than along the traditional polarity between public and private.[4]

The economy gave the initial impulse to this dynamic, when the *lex mercatoria* decoupled itself completely from national legislation, adapting laws to suit its own purposes. From then on, politics and the economy began to influence each other, blurring their original distinguishing traits and intertwining their paths inextricably. The legal voids opened by the financial markets were then filled by other types of organizations external to states and even in open competition with them, such as NGOs. Oriented more toward general humanitarian concerns than profit, NGOs are one of the most interesting experiments in innovative instituent praxis. Although formally private organizations, they pursue public goals, subordinating written rules and regulations to problems, needs, and demands that cannot be reduced to the sometimes-rigid language of state bodies. Placed at the crossroads of law, ethics, and politics, NGOs do not respond to national laws, which they often challenge, appealing instead to a kind of global civil society, undefined in law but operating *de facto* in emergency situations such as war, migration, famine, and epidemics.

Alongside these types of institutions, on the open but also fractured stage of globalization, there are others, also non-governmental, that express specific economic interests, such as the International Monetary Fund or the World Trade Organization, not to mention lobbies and corporations that are even less transparent. It goes without saying that not all institutions are equal, at times favoring vested interests and at others disadvantaged social groups. It is important not only to distinguish between them but also to take a clear stance for some against others, by adding explicitly political motivations to *dispositifs* that only seem to be purely administrative. Separating law and politics is increasingly difficult today. Even the European Union (EU), born from an act of political will but put together through legal treaties, is a mixed institution, the object of a bitter clash between various levels of overlapping and opposing sovereignties.[5]

It is worth noting[6] that in part two of *The Legal Order*, when the EU was not even remotely imaginable, Santi Romano seems to almost anticipate it in the relationship he theorizes between "original orders" and "derivative orders." Their peculiarity resides in the fact that derivative orders presuppose original orders, but the former penetrate the latter's legal spaces, altering them continuously. It would have been difficult to imagine anything more closely resembling what the institutional machinery of the EU would become. Despite its many well-known limitations, the EU remains an extraordinary testimony of instituent praxis.

The Law of Private Individuals

From the standpoint of Italian legal institutionalism, Widar Cesarini Sforza was the most acute observer of the law's profound transformation in contemporary times, opening a perspective whose possible outcomes can only be discerned today. In Cesarini Sforza's work the dissociation between law and sovereignty that Romano glimpsed but never fully theorized achieves a point of unexpected radicalization. Common to both jurists is the idea that only in the concrete order does the law finds its own space of deployment. Far from being reducible to an abstract complex of norms, the law is materially rooted in the social structure from which it emanates. Rather than establishing order, by regulating human relations or penalizing deviant behaviors, the law brings to expression a web of relations already present in the social body. Thus, it does not merely unify subjective wills through a given system of rules and regulations but reveals their originally collective aspect. Just as law always has a social character, society always has a legal undertone, inherent in every type of organization. This means that any relationship – even between two private individuals – has an institutional aspect, regardless of the public order to which it belongs. Captured at its point of emergence, relationship is the original cell of every law.[7]

This conclusion marks a fundamental divergence from Romano. The author of *The Legal Order* conceives of private relationships from the viewpoint of public law; Cesarini Sforza reverses this perspective and begins from the relationship between private individuals. Obviously, for Romano, too, private relationships can have a normative validity, but only within a public order capable of guaranteeing it. This is exactly what Cesarini Sforza disputes, namely, the dependence of private legal relationships on public ones. From this point of view, he rejects the modern idea based on a symmetry between a sovereign will at the top and individual behaviors at the bottom. The state order does affect private relationships, carving them out in different ways at various times, but it is not their normative source.

The missing element is the logical implication between the two planes of discourse: one is not the consequence of the other. From a legal viewpoint, they are mutually independent. This does not mean that the orders are equivalent in their effects on individuals; what differentiates them, though, are not different degrees of justice but the power relations that historically arise between them. The prevalence of one order over others is the factual outcome of a confrontation, or a clash, that is extra legal in nature. The categories of law should not be confused with the political categories of sovereignty, from which they are in principle autonomous. In this radically pluralistic conception – opposed to every monistic political theology – juridicity shifts from the public to the private sphere.

This does not mean that Cesarini Sforza is thinking about some sort of property law, in the sense given to it by the Romanistic tradition. *Diritto dei privati* (the law of private individuals) – as Cesarini Sforza titled his most innovative text – is not the same as "private law," which is only conceivable in relation to public law. Rather than referring to legal persons, it refers to their relationship, defined by the proportional relationship between rights and obligations. This primacy of relationship over individuals explains the introduction of a third type of law, which Cesarini Sforzo defines as "collective," placed between public and private law in a form that deconstructs "their harmony and coexistence."[8]

The author dedicates an entire section of his work to it, although without completely defining all its aspects. We know that this collective law was not foreign to the idea of Fascist corporatism, centered on an alliance between capital and labor. And yet despite this troubling association, something seems to project out of this historically compromised picture to evoke a form of "common law" or "law of the common." Cesarini Sforza provides two minimum requirements for this: on the one hand, "common" describes interests that private individuals "relate not to themselves but to the community"[9]; and on the other, interests that, rather than relating to abstract entities such as "state" and "nation," are rooted in a particular community.

All this reshapes the role of institutions in a way that is even more radical than Anglo-American neoinstitutionalism à la MacCormick.[10] Institutions are forms in which needs and social demands self-organize autonomously. The reference to a collective law, "more than private and less than public,"[11] alludes to the cooperation of subjects gathered in associations and organized in institutions. This is a marked shift with respect to the contractualist and liberal models, in a direction that brings Spinoza to mind: the transcendence of the sovereign order is replaced by the immanence of a self-organized network. Cesarini Sforza's work is traversed by a sort of materialism that seems to leave behind traditional legal formalism and penetrate the living sphere of "that vast world of goods, utilities, ends, and interests"[12] whose common denominator is a community.

· For all this to take on a new life we need to step outside the framework in which both Romano and Cesarini Sforza reasoned almost a century ago and reassemble the dialectic between law and politics that neither could theorize in his own time. To talk about a "legal order" and a "law of private individuals" can make sense only if we place these concepts in a political framework undergoing transformation. This is what the paradigm of instituent praxis refers to: the need to relocate institutions at the center of the political scene, but also to place political conflict at the center of institutions.

The end of the Second World War already marked a vindication of Anglo-American common law over continental civil law, with an associated increase in informal contracting compared to written law. Today, however, privatization processes are increasingly penetrating public law, bending it to private purposes. As Joseph A. Schumpeter foresaw in his time, capitalism has reshaped the very concept of "juridicity," not only adapting it to its own needs but giving life to new entities designed to serve transnational speculative markets. Deregulation and deformalization have long become the new rule and new form of the contemporary world. Certainly, one cannot exclude that, sooner or later, the political will react to its marginalization. But this is unlikely to mark the return of modern concepts inspired by nationalism.

In this mottled, patchwork scenario, instituent praxis takes on an ever-greater role. Let us begin from the legal point of view. Never have legal battles and battles over the law appeared so open and uncertain. They can legitimize existing power relations or work toward their transformation. They can favor advantaged social groups or those that are increasingly marginalized and impoverished. They can shut down borders or extend bridges. In any case, the law never plays a purely formal, neutral role – an idea relegated by now to old legal textbooks. We might as well take note of its instituent potential and guide it in a direction that is conducive to new relationships.

———

This requires an explanation of the constituent function that the law has always, surreptitiously, performed.
Italian institutionalism – from Romano to Costantino
Mortati – has already traced the law back to its living
roots. Now it is a matter of giving them a clearer political
significance. Politics, it has been said, is not the simple
expression of the social but its institution, through
recognizing the conflictual lines that cut through it and
taking positions in their regard. This is the only way
that institution, law, and politics will rediscover, at the
end of the modern era, the constitutive relationship that
marked their birth.

Subversive Justice

The relationship between law and politics – the politicization of the law – does not necessarily have to
pass through the centrality of the state. On the contrary, it can come from the fragmentation of the
legal system into a series of institutions located outside the state's orbit. This is the path taken by the
legal sociologist Gunther Teubner. A scholar of Niklas
Luhmann's systems theory, he takes his cue from the
radical decentering of constitutionalization processes
that have impacted contemporary society. Teubner
believes that these dynamics can no longer be analyzed
using the conceptual tools of European public law; they
must be related to a form of "state-less constitutionalism."[13] Even the traditional appeal to international
institutions appears inadequate to him, since they still
refer to the relationship between the sovereign rights
of the various states. But the idea of something like
a world constitution, in a heterogeneous geopolitical

context like the one we live in today, is equally untenable.

What, then? The only practicable avenue is to recognize a multiplicity of social constitutions, neither entirely public nor entirely private, created in the various spheres that differentiate contemporary society: science, technology, media, medicine, education, transportation, and so forth. By now the distinction between public and private has been outstripped by a polycontextuality that is irreducible to a binary logic, because it has been divided up into a constellation of semantic worlds that run perpendicular to the classic modern dichotomies. If anything, the distinction between public and private, broken off from that between state and society, resurfaces within each sector, creating an effect of continual, conflictual tensions.

A first type of conflict is that between the laws of individual national states and the continuously morphing rules of the new postnational aggregations. Other types of disagreement also arise, however, between individual interests and transnational enterprises. At their center lies the problematic notion of "human rights," situated in the yawning chasm between law and justice. Violations of fundamental rights by transnational companies regarding working conditions or environmental pollution are well known. To these must be added the lethal damage caused by pharmaceutical companies who, by raising the prices of life-saving medicines, indirectly condemn to death entire groups of people living in the planet's most impoverished areas.

This is a blatant violation of fundamental rights. How can we remedy this? And, before that, how are we to define the parties involved, in legal terms?

Because multinationals do not have any specific legal personhood, it is difficult for them to be charged with a crime; but it is also complicated for indistinct populations to gain any recognition of subjectivity. The basic problem is that the only vocabulary available to legal language is that of personhood. It is difficult to arraign an anonymous process, such as air pollution, for which, apparently, no one is directly responsible. Thus, our much-proclaimed human rights remain stuck on paper – when they are not exploited, that is, for other purposes, as has often happened.

In short, the gap between rights and justice remains dramatically wide. What prevents it from being bridged is precisely the autopoietic character of the different social systems, that is, their lack of external references. While this is true of every system, it is especially true of the rigidly formalized system of the law. As Luhmann argues, the law performs an immune function, a neutralizing role, in conflicts that affect society. But this neutralization is precisely what separates it from justice, which, on the contrary, requires that we take a stance against injustice, even a confrontational one, wherever it lurks.

This "partiality," founded on general norms, is what the law cannot express. If it did, if it spoke the language of the common instead of the language of immunity, it would overlap onto politics, thereby losing its specificity. After all, a real encounter between law and politics has never taken place in Western history. The pathways of *nomos* have never met up with those of *dike*, just as the Roman tradition of *ius* never truly joined up with the Greek tradition of the *polis*. This lack of integration is a wound that cuts through the entire history of the West, dividing it into two asymmetrical fronts. The formalism of the law has never been integrated with the political struggle for justice.[14]

In "Self-Subversive Justice: Contingency or Transcendence Formula of Law?" Teubner follows a genealogical agenda in tracing the impossible relation between law and justice.[15] Although the law is aware of its historical "injustices," there can be no legal theory of justice. On the contrary, justice constitutes the outside, or the transcendence, of law, that which it can never attain from inside its own protocols. But if this closes the door on an affirmative definition of "justice," it does not preclude the possibility, and the necessity, of a critical self-examination of the law. The law can approach justice only in negative terms, as what it is not and can never become, recognizing its own impassable limit. It can try to right wrongs, of course, but using its own procedures only for particular cases.

After all, its ultimate political resource resides in the particular. It is a matter of abandoning a general, totalizing conception of politics, which has sunk with the modern concepts that inspired it, giving rise to the proliferation of institutions we now have before us. Regardless of nationalistic resurgences, this proliferation makes it impossible to ever return to the old state-centric models. Equally impossible to imagine, however, is a globalization without borders. We need, rather, to make the most of the multiplicity in play, by structuring the variety of institutional languages in a "Leibnizian" network of independent, interrelated monads.

One could view this project of systemic differentiation as a form of depoliticization; but only if one has a nineteenth-century paradigm of politics in mind. What needs to be done, rather, is to restore a sense of concreteness to political activity inside the individual institutions. We need to support this differentiation process, working across the lines of tension that run between and within the various social subsystems. A possible connection between law and justice must be found in the dialectic between particular and general interests. Such a connection will be manifested not by a unified order but by the autonomy of the individual, self-organized structures. Devoid of any totalizing ambitions, the political will be the expression of the intrinsic normativity of the individual sectors.

From this point of view, the "law of private individuals" will coincide with the autonomous sphere of multiple institutions, thus reforging a new relationship with public law. "Public," from this point of view, is what allows and stimulates democratization processes in the distinctly articulated spheres of technology, economy, education, healthcare, and so on. To bring about an increasingly inclusive democracy, sociocultural conflicts need to be activated in each of them. This democratization process can and must include the participation of NGOs, union structures, and professional orders, allied in the construction of a common law, which, if it cannot attain justice, can at least project its icon onto the plural multiplicity of society.

Is this a convincing analysis? Can it be exported outside the most developed Western enclaves? And, above all, is it consistent with a viable, impactful political project? Several uncertainties remain to be addressed. Let us say that between a post-Hobbesian politics, which can no longer be reactivated, and a post-Spinozist politics, still to come, the Leibnizian *ars combinatoria* that Teubner proposes does open a vista. In it, institutions are pivotal meeting points, where the threads of law and politics, long kept separate, begin to interlace once again on a post-state horizon.

Beyond the State?

Obviously, when I talk about a "post-state horizon" I do not mean a world without nations. After the state – it is fair to say – there is still the state. A similar observation can be made about sovereignty, which is stressed, exhausted, challenged by the processes of deconstitutionalization, but still present and operating all around the globe, in different ways and degrees. We must avoid projecting what is happening in Europe, albeit amid delays and contradictions – a stingy yielding of sovereignty to the Union – onto the rest of the world, which is still solidly organized around the pillar of sovereignty. As should be noted, sovereignty does not signify only domination, closure, and exclusion but also democracy, rights, and equality. It would be a historical and political mistake to deny the complexity and depth of "sovereignty," how the concept has taken shape and changed from the medieval period to today, or to confuse it with the media caricature that for some years now has been known as "sovereignism."[16]

After all, after questioning whether institutions are necessarily state-like in character, it would be difficult to exclude the state from their ranks. We need to guard against a binary schema that opposes the state order to the global order, or sovereignty to government, without realizing that they are not only inextricably intertwined but historically inscribed within each other. Then again, as economic historians know well, it is impossible to separate the birth and development of capitalism from the state container in which they took place historically, expanding the container to the point of deforming it, true, but never bursting its seams.

This applies more generally to the relationship between politics and the economy, which can never be attributed to a "zero sum" game, since even the depoliticization processes that favor the global economy have a political origin and outcome.[17] What else but the state produced the structural conditions for economic primacy starting in the late 1970s, by diminishing or suspending governmental control over the organization of the labor market? And was neoliberalism, in all its forms, including German ordoliberalism, not also born from a political choice of the Atlantic and Central European states, quickly followed by almost all the others? The phenomenon of denationalization also originated from within states, along with the opposing, outdated attempts at renationalization that we have been witnessing in recent years. And does contemporary neomercantilism, with its increased duties on imported goods, not have a clear geopolitical origin? Does it not respond to hegemonic challenges with an obviously political nature? States themselves have organized their own "impolitical" withdrawal from the praxis of capital.

The question can also be looked at from another angle, in a more dynamic dialectic, that views states as a significant battleground between powers and counterpowers. While in the last half century states appear to have yielded both to local interests and to transnational networks, in the preceding 30 years, during the "glorious" period of welfare construction,[18] they were a fundamental terrain for class conflict. As recently as the first 20 years of the new millennium, in Latin America, Spain, Greece, and elsewhere, the governments of these countries were targets of a political battle between opposing social forces that gave rise to highly innovative constituent processes. This means that state institutions, and the state itself as an institution, can be used in different and contrasting ways: as a site for the accumulation of political power by dominant groups, but also for a change in power relations in favor of the less advantaged.

It is true that many of the constitutional experiments within states have failed or regressed in the face of internal and external pressures. From North Africa to Brazil, they have given rise to a series of authoritarian backlashes, at the same time as Greece was bowing to the diktat of the Troika. This demonstrates that, although still in operation, national sovereignty does not have the strength to victoriously oppose the "operations" of capital. This makes highly problematic what some define as "leftwing sovereignism," which is often united with a populist rhetoric inclined to mythicize a people's homogeneity that ends up neutralizing social conflict. Despite not quitting the stage, then, the state lacks the force to be the fulcrum of a challenge to transnational economic powers, unless it plays at the same level as them, by connecting to a wider network of non-state institutions. Of course, as far as a possible political transformation is concerned, not all states and governments are equivalent. But such a transformation is bound to grind to a halt or regress if locked inside the tiny fort of established state institutions.

———

Étienne Balibar spoke recently of a "Machiavelli theorem,"[19] alluding to an expansion of democracy through a constitutionalization of conflicts at the height of the social confrontation that courses through contemporary society. In a country that still lacked a national state, as did Italy at the time, Machiavelli saw politics as the source of life in the interrupted dialectic of order and conflict: not one against the other, but one inside the other. Conflictual order and ordered conflict were, for him, the two sides of a vital potency that makes itself into institution, not only in state bodies but in every social relationship. Laws, military forces, and religions are the original institutions out of which all others are born before converging into the state. But even after state formation, these institutions continue to produce politics.

Once the communal experiment ended with the constitution of absolute states, only at times, and for rare moments, did the instituent paradigm resurface in modern history. After the age of revolutions, a resurgence can be recognized at the end of World War II: first, when a number of constitutions were written, including the Italian one, and the foundations of the European Union were laid in the Ventotene Manifesto; secondly, during the subsequent "Glorious Thirty Years" – the postwar economic boom period – when worker parties and unions performed the "tribunitian" role in republican institutions that Machiavelli had described. They worked by putting the spheres of politics, the economy, and society into relation and tension, making labor and civil rights a political issue and politics a social issue. Today, even that glorious era is behind us, as is the entire twentieth century,[20] without having left any heirs worthy of that epithet. This calls for a new instituent engagement, along two distinct and yet converging lines. In both cases, they connect inside and outside, without erasing the distinction between them.

The first involves the relationship between public and private institutions, which are dialecticized to some degree under the concept of "common." As Pierre Dardot and Christian Laval have argued in a book making frequent reference to the instituent paradigm, "common"[21] should not be understood as a good or as a set of goods or even as a community, regardless of how this is defined. Common is the cooperative form of instituent praxis as creation – at once social, legal, and political – of new instituent processes, which endure in time through associations, organizations, and networks, destined to widen the circle of social inclusion in each sphere.

The second, still to be put into action, runs between political organizations in different countries – especially in the European region, in our case – united by common goals of a civil, social, and environmental nature. Here, too, instead of existing institutions – parties, unions, and parliamentary groups – it is a matter of instituting new bodies capable of taking over from the depleted twentieth-century liberal, popular, and socialist political families that still sit in the European Parliament. None of them seem up to the challenges we are facing. From this point of view, too, the current pandemic offers a crucial testing ground not only for national and transnational institutions but for the instituent thought that is maturing in various epicenters of contemporary reflection.

———

V
Institutions and Biopolitics

Biopolitics

As we end our journey, let us return to the expression *vitam instituere* with which we began. What does it mean to institute life? Does life allow itself to be instituted? Or is life what penetrates the sphere of institutions and regenerates them? The issue under debate in these questions, quite clearly, is the relationship between life and politics that for some time now has been put under the rubric of "biopolitics." A question arises in its regard, however, concerning contemporary political thought. How do the paradigms of institution and biopolitics relate – and, before that, are they compatible? Or are their conceptual lexicons too heterogeneous to be integrated? Personally, I believe it is not only possible but necessary to work at their point of intersection. The current pandemic, which forms the inevitable backdrop for these reflections, serves as a reminder of the need for this dual approach.

The fact that the pandemic is situated on a biopolitical horizon is plain for all to see. Never have the paths of politics and life intertwined as during this crisis, with highly problematic and still uncertain results, because the biological life of entire populations has been threatened by the virus. It goes without saying that there have been other things at stake too: community, freedom, and the economy. But the fact remains that Covid-19 first attacked our survival, giving rise to a series of patently biopolitical measures. The medical and social initiatives to obtain immunity, implemented all over the world, have this sort of biopolitical tone. Indeed, it can be said that never as in these circumstances has the immunological core of contemporary biopolitics been revealed, in its most pronounced form. The state of emergency, or exception, that has been talked about so much – a bit overblown at times – should be traced to the same paradigm: extra legal measures are only justified by the defense of life.

The biopolitical character of the pandemic crisis has not excluded institutional intervention but rather required it, putting institutions to the test and leaving them changed in the process. This is precisely what calls for an instituent praxis that measures up to the situation. Time will tell whether and to what degree it will be put into effective action. The fact remains that from the smallest to the largest – from local health authorities to the European Union – every institution has produced changes within its organization. In the real world, in short, biopolitics and institutions are complementary sides of the same process. But if the two paradigms are firmly clasped together in practice, their integration appears to be less fluid in the realm of theory. There remains the perception of a gap, a hiatus, creating a distance between things that in reality are close. In the realm of concepts, biopolitics and institutions belong to different semantic fields that, at least in appearance, are extraneous to each other.

Where does this feeling of heterogeneity originate from? Let us begin with a widespread definition. It is often said that "biopolitics" must entail a direct implication between politics and biological life that bypasses any institutional mediation. The truth is more complex than this, in the sense that for any immediacy to last in time, it must always pass through some form of institutionalization. And, indeed, this is what happens in all biopolitical procedures, including the urgent state of exception: it, too, was necessarily implemented by means of institutional *dispositifs*.

The fact that this is not entirely obvious, or even remains obscured, probably stems from a conceptual discrepancy between the biopolitical and institutional lexicons that issues from the way Michel Foucault developed the concept of "biopolitics." This is not the place to reconstruct the steps he took, even in broad strokes, but it can be said that his theoretical "allergy" to institutional discourse arises from the prevalently anti-juridical tone of his entire body of work, especially at the time of his biopolitical turn. In the concluding section of *The Will to Knowledge*, where the new concept is introduced, Foucault writes that "the existence in question is no longer the juridical existence of sovereignty; at stake is the biological existence of a population."[1] As always, his perspective is happily ambivalent. On the one hand, his critique of the sovereign apparatus is in tune with instituent thought; on the other, his distancing from the juridical realm ultimately drags institutions into a cone of shadow too.

As Foucault states in the same book, when the sovereign regime is exhausted, biopower no longer relates to subjects of the law but to living beings, who are formed as individuals by disciplines of the body, and in the public realm by social control. This transition to a new phase is marked by the biopolitical *dispositif* of norms, which take the place of the juridical system of the law. This does not mean that the institutions of justice disappear, but they are increasingly incorporated into a continuum of medical and administrative apparatuses that, for the most part, fulfill a normalizing function. For this reason, continues Foucault, what we have is a phase of juridical regression. The laws, constitutions, and codes originating from the period of the French Revolution had the function of concealing behind their clamorous exhibitions an essentially regulatory power. From then on "it was life more than the law that became the issue of political struggles, even if the latter were formulated through affirmations concerning rights."[2]

The striking aspect about these assertions is the disconnection, or opposition even, between the speres of life and law that somehow does not fit into the very paradigm of biopolitics. The moment politics directly impacts biological life, empowering its development, the juridical devices of the law tend to be replaced by norms, which are more malleable and pervasive. But where are norms to be found, it could be objected, if not in the shifting framework of institutions: administration, education, healthcare, family, religion, sexuality? The problem evidently lies in the broader or narrower definition of "institution." Without going into too much detail, it can be said that between the two poles of sovereignty and life, Foucault associates institutions with the former, in opposition to the latter. Despite the biopolitical turn, or precisely because of it, he leaves unexplored the place where institutions and life intersect. Institutions discipline life; they keep watch over it and select it, but they do not empower it. Similarly, at the other corner of the quadrant, life does not bathe institutions: it abandons them to their closure.

There is something in this parting of ways that affects the very concept of "biopolitics," putting it at odds with a contemporary condition that, in other respects, it fully explicates. Ever since the notion of biopolitics was first developed, it has apparently contained an element of ambivalence or even indecisiveness regarding the definition of "life" as it relates to "politics." My impression is that Foucault conceived of the two poles of "biopolitics" – *bios* and politics – separately rather than as a single semantic block. Only later did he join them together in a way that ultimately causes one to overlap and, therefore, also subordinate the other. Life is either seized by a power destined to exercise violence on it; or politics is deformed and, ultimately, outdone by a life that is antagonistic to any formal constraint. Following Foucault's formulation of the term, these are the two tendencies to which the paradigm of biopolitics has remained vulnerable, as both cause and effect of the conceptual rupture between life and institution. The figure of power is what separates them so drastically. The moment power appears to appropriate institutions, employing them to control and dominate life, all life can do is oppose them head-on. But at that point, with no embankments to contain it, the flow of life risks losing its relationship with both institutions and politics.

Double Birth

The blind spot of contemporary political philosophy remains the failed encounter between institutions and life: the elusiveness of that *institutio vitae* emblazoned on the entranceway to Western legal civilization. For Foucault, as we have seen, life can expand only when it is outside the oppressive cage of institutions; for Hannah Arendt, on the contrary, institutions must be protected from the pressure of life. But it must be recognized that Arendt gave us the twentieth century's most powerful instituent thought. All her work converges in a commitment to build political institutions capable of withstanding the impact of time – but outside the sovereign regime that is accepted as an unquestioned presupposition by a large part of modern political thought.

The originality of her perspective compared to her surrounding philosophical milieu can be judged precisely on this basis, but also on its divergence from the biopolitical semantic field, which Arendt does use, but in the negative, so to speak – by considering its risks rather than its opportunities. More distant than ever from the Hobbesian paradigm of order, Arendt does not even agree with the paradigm of government, which is still monistic in tone. For her, political action is instead structured in a widespread network of institutions that cannot be reduced to a single point of command. Remote from all contractualist theories – including Rousseau's democratic one – which presuppose the homogeneity of the people, Arendt identifies herself with the separation of powers principle that runs from Montesquieu to American federalism. To prevent power from amassing inordinately, institutions must be multiple and different from each other.

Arendt's focus, however, more than on institutional mechanisms or individual institutions, is on the instituent principle per se. The reason American federalism has withstood growing depoliticization longer than European countries is because the founding fathers placed the principle of legitimacy in the act of foundation itself, thereby safeguarding the connection between permanence and change evoked by the intrinsic meaning of institutions. The fact that even the American constitution yielded at a certain point to the return of sovereignty is the effect of a regressive wave that, according to Arendt, affects modern politics as a whole. In her interpretation, no political experience is spared a negative judgment.

This impasse is the result of an imbalance between instituent and instituted, tipped toward the former: for Arendt, politics coincides to such a degree with the creation of the *novum* that, in a continuous proliferation of beginnings, it loses any form of stability. None of the characteristics she assigns to political action – plurality, irreversibility, novelty – can ensure its permanence in time. Instituent logic is so radicalized that it concentrates all political action in the instant of its birth. Of the two meanings of the Greek *archein* – "to begin" and "to command" – only the former, corresponding to the Latin *agere*, is emphasized: "Because they are *initium*, newcomers and beginners by virtue of birth, men take initiative, are prompted into action."[3] This instituent power characterizes history, which "has many beginnings but no end"[4]; but also, even more so, political action, which "is essentially always the beginning of something new."[5]

Nevertheless, the birth she talks about is not the biological one – headed inevitably, like all natural processes, toward death. On the contrary, the act of radical renewal eludes the natural cycle, ushering in an experience that is symbolic in nature. The psychoanalyst and legal historian Pierre Legendre – who locates the term *vitam instituere* at the origins of Western history – argues that it is a second birth, whose meaning is concentrated specifically in its difference from the first birth.[6] This is where we see an opposition in principle between institution and biological life.

The dissonance between Arendt's perspective and Foucault's is evident. For her, biological life impinges on politics only to destitute it; just as politics only remains such until it is absorbed by biological life. One begins where the other finishes, and vice versa. The human activity of politics is removed from the urgency of life's necessities, so much so that when life invades it, it shrivels up and retreats. This is what happened to the French Revolution, pushing it toward self-destruction – a tendency avoided by the American Revolution because it was not burdened by the pressure of natural needs and remained within the institutional dialectic. Unlike the American revolutionaries, who from the beginning aimed at "the foundation of freedom and the establishment of lasting institutions,"[7] the French Jacobins surrendered to biological necessity, simultaneously sacrificing politics and institutions. From then on, instead of joining together in a virtuous circle, biological life and instituent praxis have taken turns negating each other: as one grows, the other shrinks.

At the origin of this divarication is the Christian notion that life is sacred, becoming the supreme good to which all others must be sacrificed. This primacy was maintained even after modern secularization, which replaced the permanence of the body politic with the survival of the individual. Thus, what is most mortal – an individual life – was elevated to the highest rank, long occupied by the city and its institutions. With the process of socialization that started in late modernity, the life of the individual then became an integral part of a single natural flow, coinciding with the development of the human species as a whole. It was then that all human activities, previously distinct from one another, were mobilized in defense of this single living process, resulting in a depoliticization that washed over all society.

The French Revolution is generally seen as the beginning of modern politics, but, in reality, it was caught in this regressive dynamic that replaced the pursuit of liberty with a preoccupation for survival. In this exchange between freedom and life, the principle of the political was destroyed, along with the institutions that embody it. From then on, biological life became the unstoppable tide that has sunk political action. In a word, institutions and life are shown once again to be incompatible, facing off in a clash that subordinates one to the domination of the other, albeit with the parts reversed. Whereas Foucault criticizes institutions because they repress the free flow of life, Arendt views biological life as an irresistible force that ruins institutions, leading them into violence.

Impersonal Law

How can we restore the connection between institutions and life, overcoming the theoretical and political deadlock that barred its expression throughout the twentieth century? Let us start from the first side of the question, that is, the oft-repeated need to "give life" to institutions, in both senses of instituting and revitalizing them.

As a matter of fact, the idea of a "living law,"[8] such that it not only governs life but also includes it in its procedures, is not entirely new. Although its mention dates to the origins of the Western tradition, in Greek tragedy and pre-Platonic philosophy, the formula appears in European legal culture at the beginning of the twentieth century, particularly in the work of Eugen Ehrlich.[9] For Ehrlich, a sociologist of law, a "living law" does not arise out of legal scholarship or legislation but from the concreteness of social practices. Accordingly, the expression *corpus iuris* (body of laws) must be interpreted literally: not as a set of laws to be applied to the social body but as the embodiment of the social fact in the law. Understood in these terms, the life *of* the law is also life *in* the law.

Following in the wake of Carl von Savigny, Ehrlich not only asserts the historicity of the movement of life, he instills it into history. This is the source of his dispute with Hans Kelsen. Equating law with state, Kelsen posits the unity of the legal form; Ehrlich takes his cue instead from the plurality of concrete legal experiences, without gathering them into a single order. The importance he gives to constitution goes in the "existential" direction, so to speak, of instituted lifeforms that precede the law.

Compared to Kelsen's formalism, constitution is a concrete, vital, effective sphere that exists prior to any other jurisdiction and shapes it based on extra legal demands. There are real situations – such as an unmarried couple living together or undocumented foreign workers in a given territory – that somehow require a law, even though they have yet to be juridified. Of course, whether they do pass from a non-juridical to a juridical status cannot be taken for granted, but it hinges on a confrontation, or clash, between opposing interests. For this reason, living law is always potentially conflictual: it fights *in* the law and *for* the law. The law fights inside and outside its own boundaries to extend its range of action to previously excluded areas.

This inclusionary tendency of living law – and of the institutions in which it materializes – has led to talk of a "common law" or a "law of the common,"[10] as we have seen in the previous chapter. Its affirmative definition remains problematic, but a negative one is easier to arrive at. A common law is neither the simple extension of public law nor the pure opposite of private law; nor should it be understood, however, as a point of mediation between the two. Grasping its essence requires that we adopt a longitudinal viewpoint, going beyond the canonic dichotomy between public and private and, even before that, beyond the legal lexicon itself, nudging it in a direction that is apparently outside the language of law. We must do so, because "law" and "common" are contradictory in principle: the law, as such, lies outside the semantic field of community and is inscribed instead in that of immunity.

Not surprisingly, Niklas Luhmann defined law as "the immune subsystem" of social systems. It acts as an immune system in the sense that it protects society from reciprocal violence purely by threatening its own violent penalty. As in all immune processes, we protect ourselves from harm by absorbing a sustainable part of what ails us. Additionally, the law is an immune device because, even if it aims to be fully inclusive, it necessarily presupposes the possibility of exclusion. A law that is common, that truly belongs to everyone, would not be law in the strictest sense of the word; for those who benefit from it to perceive it as such – as a right and not as a given – they must in any case assume that someone cannot benefit from it. In logical terms, only exclusion, whether real or possible, gives meaning to inclusion. And, in historical terms, the fact that a right has been granted or won at a given time means that it can always be lost if the forces that established it succumb to other opposing ones that demand its repeal.

This explains why no matter how hard we try to identify, or even envisage, a "common law," it remains a complicated task – because either it is law, which is to say, a set of prerogatives of some against others, or it is common, which is to say, inimical to any particular prerogative. Of course, "common law" could also be understood more narrowly as the enlargement of a legal space or, vice versa, as the reduction of exclusion. Think, for example, about the granting of citizenship to some foreign residents in a given territory – to some, that is, on the basis of certain conditions and never to all. From this more limited point of view, action can be taken on the one hand by encouraging the institutional self-organization of movements, and on the other by working on constitutionalizing social processes that are not originally constitutional.

———

The precondition for both processes is a governmental practice committed in full to social, environmental, and healthcare needs that serve the interests of as many people as possible. The areas for action are myriad: from redistributing resources to constructing protected ecosystems, rebuilding public healthcare systems, and bolstering the education and research sectors. It is a matter of reintroducing, but also profoundly reconfiguring, the logic of welfare after it was dismantled by neoliberalism between the 1970s and the 1980s – but with the difference, compared to classic welfare, of extending its scope beyond the framework of the now inadequate state horizon.

Institutional pluralism must be brought back into play and, before that, a flexible, decentered instituent praxis, one that is aware of the conflicts that cut through society and is ready to take part in them. This means taking a political stance, inside and outside institutions. A law that defines itself as "common" must necessarily throw itself into the fray between opposing interests and take sides. Rights do not dwell in some overhanging realm and then drop down into jurisdictions. They do not exist outside of history – in nature or in the legislator's mind – waiting to become historicized. They are points of internal tension in the legal system that at a certain moment break its formal chains, creating a new, *de facto* system, also destined to change under the pressure of further points of insurgence.

To identify the intersecting lines between institutions and life, perhaps we should speak of an "impersonal law" rather than a "common law." We have already seen how the new instituent praxis leaves behind the legal lexicon of personhood, both at the level of the individual and at that of the state. Going beyond the modern dichotomy between public and private law toward a new legal semantics presupposes that we abandon, or at least profoundly remodel, the traditional personalist lexicon. From this point of view, "impersonal" may be more appropriate than "common" to signal a change of course toward a new law that is neither public nor private.

This philosophy of the impersonal recognizes its genetic moment in Averroes's reflections on the possible intellect, placed outside the individual mind, in a space that is open to the entire human community. Authors such as Giordano Bruno, Spinoza, and Schelling, up to Foucault, and Deleuze, each take up this perspective in their own way, along a line that in recent years has been developed especially in Italy.[11] This current of thought has most recently been picked up and elaborated on with originality by the historian of Roman law Aldo Schiavone, in a wide-ranging book on the idea of "equality."[12] His basic thesis is that the time has come to detach it from the historical and anthropological form of individuality that has characterized modernity as a whole, without, however, tipping it toward a collectivist notion of "sociality." As Simone Weil, perhaps the greatest thinker of the impersonal, taught, the social is nothing more than the mass projection of the individual, whose paradigmatic blueprint it shares.[13]

I and *we* – both first persons, singular and plural – must be replaced, if need be, by the third person of *he / she* or *it*, which, as the great linguist Émile Benveniste put it, is the *non-person*, or the person of the impersonal.[14] Without being able to explore this topic in as much detail as it deserves, we can clearly see how it relates to the mode of instituent praxis, freed from the subject-person mechanism to foster a transindividual form of subjectivity. Of course, it is no easy task to translate this impersonal law into institutions that give a central place to creating an effective equality, or to imagine the status of institutions that are impersonal because they stand outside the legal lexicon of person-hood. But it is from here, from this narrow ridge, that there emerges a new inquiry on the character of justice, at once universal and common.

Instituting Life

The revitalization of institutions only addresses one aspect of the issue, however. It explains the first facet of the relationship – a possible and necessary one – between institutions and life: the energetic charge that institutions can and, increasingly, must absorb from life. This first facet must cross over into the other, related to the institution of life itself,[15] to the institutional trait that is vested in *bios* from the beginning. In the expression *institutio vitae* from which we started, life is both the subject and object of institution: it is instituent and instituted at the same time. This is where, from this side, biopolitics makes its reappearance. The very fact that *bios* – and not *zoe*, not pure living matter – is spoken of means that human life has always and in all cases been instituted, that is, inscribed in a historical and symbolic fabric from which it cannot be separated. The institution of life – its placement on a particular horizon of meaning – is not a subjective option available to us but a given, which qualifies human life with respect to all other living species. As we have said, every life is suspended between two joined but not superimposable births: the first is biological and the second symbolic in character, coinciding with the use of language.

Already at the dawn of biology, the French physiologist Xavier Bichat spoke about two lives in human life: one unreflective and purely reproductive, and the other relational, equipped for higher functions. Although the first prevails quantitatively over the second, without the latter our life would not be human; it would lose its qualifying element, sliding into an indistinct stratum of life. Therefore, the expression "bare life" (*blosse Leben*) should not be understood as something real, or simply possible, but as a logical point necessary to identify the "qualified life"; not unlike the concept, equally unfindable in reality, of a "state of nature," which has served to define, by contrast, the civil state. Just as there has never been a purely natural human being, so too there has never been a life that is completely stripped of its formal characteristics – not even in the extreme situation of the extermination camps. Even when reduced to its lowest level and facing imminent death, until it is extinguished, life remains a form of life.

For good reason, the expression "bare life" was never used by Foucault, because despite the interpretations later forced on his concept of "biopolitics," it always remained anchored to history. Nonetheless, especially in some of the most influential interpretations, there remains an imbalance in the conception of "biopolitics," something unspoken regarding the very notion of "life." This is a possible tendency that overlays life on top of itself, leaving it devoid of historical and institutional determinants. We know that at a certain point in his studies, Foucault opened a window onto the reversal of biopolitics, into a form of "thanatopolitics," revealed at its most extreme point in Nazism. But if we read his pages carefully, the horror brought to culmination by Nazism was not caused by life's withdrawal or by some limit that constrains life within certain confines; on the contrary, it resulted from life being unleashed beyond all limits. Nazism always called on the absolute primacy of a life unfettered by any limiting conditions, as an irresistible force. This extreme will to life, emancipated from any form and synonymous with a force, is precisely what flipped over into its opposite. The moment life is absolutized to the point of wanting nothing but itself, sweeping away any differences within itself, it ends up destroying everything that it imagines as opposed to it and, ultimately, even itself.

Picking up the threads of our discussion, it may well be said that this catastrophic outcome results from the breakdown between life and institution: between life as force and life as form. A completely deinstitutionalized life, one that is utterly coextensive with itself, is destined sooner or later to implode from an excess of immanence – as both Heidegger and Levinas argued, from opposing sides. What is racism, for that matter, if not an idea of life flattened entirely onto the bodily plane or made equivalent to the color of the skin? Modern and contemporary history offers more than a few examples of this possible biological deviation. Were all the expansionist wars of the last two centuries not waged in the name of life, for that "vital space" evoked by all European colonial ventures, before being appropriated by the Nazi ideology and culminating in genocide? And are our current ecological disasters not also due to an unbridled anthropocentrism, which, once again, in the name of human life sacrifices the life of the world? The major exponents of European philosophy grasped this risk but did not always manage to keep it at bay.[16] The "will to life" was the watchword that, albeit in different versions, connected the philosophies of Schopenhauer and Nietzsche along the same axis, in both cases courting the risk of turning into their opposites. At its apex, when life is an absolute, freed from all constraints, it can only flow back toward death.

The person who went the farthest in acknowledging this fact, and was almost overwhelmed by it, was Freud. Projecting his gaze beyond the pleasure principle, he opened a door onto our modern knowledge of life that, to the end, he remained reluctant to go through. But, in the same text, when he concludes that the sentinels of life coincide with the guardians of death, the inextricable connection between the two comes to light in sinister flashes. Even Henri Bergson's *élan vital*, which represents the acme of twentieth-century vitalism, is fueled by the deaths of individuals, which serves the total vital flow. The living and the dying pass into each other in a single vital process, which, given the material that feeds it, can also be defined as deadly.

This is the outcome of an affirmation of life that, by denying the negative that inhabits it, is ultimately devoured by it. A life devoid of folds, scansions, and differences that mark out its rhythm risks slipping into a whirlpool with no embankments. The thinker who pushed Bergson's vital process to its boiling point, arriving at a sort of absolute immanence – I am referring to Deleuze – was forced to recognize that the flow of desire contains lines of death and destruction that direct it against the same life from which it issues. Contrary to common belief, there is an obscure relationship between extreme vitalism and thought on death, as if one were the background out of which the other is cut. Even Foucault, before arriving at his own recognition of biopolitics, acknowledged that "it is from the depth of their lives that death overtakes living beings."[17]

To such an absolute life – entirely immanent to itself – instituent thought opposes the symbolic character of a human existence inscribed in the fabric of its own historicity. Earlier we talked about the idea of the "impersonal," needed to deconstruct the metaphysics of personhood; the emphasis should now be placed on the difference, and on the distance, that makes every life irreducibly unique: *a* life, *that* life. "Impersonal" does not mean "undifferentiated": on the contrary, it arises from the valuing of differences. For differences to remain such, they need institutions to safeguard them from the pervasiveness of global flows and automatic apparatuses. We need to reconnect the function of life to its instituted form, understood as the way that each life is conducted, always in a singular fashion. Foucault's last writings on the government of self appear to follow this lead, orienting biopolitics in an instituent direction absent from his previous texts. After binding life to the semantics of force, according to a Nietzschean inspiration, it is as if his thinking felt a need for form: the need for each person to at least institute his or her own life.

It seems to me that this is precisely the task of contemporary philosophy, if there is such a thing: not to oppose the instituent paradigm to the biopolitical one, or substitute the instituent with the biopolitical, but to integrate them in a way that is productive for both. Never more than today has the biopolitical project that Foucault inaugurated in the mid-1970s shown its hermeneutic capacity in interpreting contemporary phenomenology. But the concept of biopolitics must be rethought to overcome the underlying divide between what appears to some as an absolute power over life and to others as a life free of all power. Instituent thought is intended to heal this fracture, a primarily philosophical rather than political one.

Ever since the concept of biopolitics first appeared, it has been tied to the fall of institutional mediations in favor of a direct implication between politics and life. But this definition presupposed, on the one hand, the static character of institutions, viewed as incapable of incorporating vital processes; and, on the other, a notion of "life" conceived as resistant to recognizing its dual character: instituent and instituted. From this, in the void of living institutions, came the opposition between a politics oppressive to life and a life incapable of meeting up with politics. Only by considering life as always already formed can institutions incorporate its vital force. Only in this way will force and form, life and institutions, nature and history recognize their original unity. And only then will the enigmatic term *vitam institutere* reveal to us something about its still hidden meaning.

Epilogue

Let me try to summarize what I have written. Like every genealogical study, this one also moves between the two poles of actuality and origins, using one as the angle from which to examine the other. I have therefore probed the role that institutions played in the epidemic emergency, starting from a term with uncertain but very ancient origins that refers to the institution of life. The idea that life must start a new cycle after a tragic phase of existential contraction rings as true today as it does in all other periods. When past and present are seen from this point of view, they appear remarkably contemporaneous, despite their historical distance. And this is why they can illuminate each other. The history of the institution offers an ideal illustration of this principle. There is a deep connection between the interpretation often associated with the concept of institution – a closed and defensive one – and its medieval origin, especially as expressed in canon law. In contrast to Roman juridical practice, it subordinates the institution to a natural order imposed by divine will.

Epilogue

Even after modern secularization, it continued to be portrayed according to this top-down conception, through a paradigm of order passed from Hobbes to Weber and beyond. This reductive interpretation has marked discussion on the topic in political philosophy since the 1960s, splitting it into a stark opposition between institutions and movements, a division whose effects we are still paying for to this day. Only recently has a new space of research been opened for thought, which has taken the name "instituent." Anticipated by some little-read currents of twentieth-century thought – a particular branch of French sociology, German philosophical anthropology, and Italian legal institutionalism – it shifts the emphasis from instituted order to instituent praxis. Along these lines, the state – long considered by definition to be the institutional center of gravity – becomes one institution among others, challenged by them on all grounds.

Compared to positive law, constructed around the *dispositif* of the legal person, the institutional dynamic has taken other paths, cutting across the modern dichotomies of public and private, individual and society, preservation and innovation. Institutional praxis reinterprets the relationship between continuity and discontinuity in a new way, leaving behind both progressive historicism and the revolutionary tradition of *ex nihilo* creation: nothing is born from nothing, but every institution can also radically modify the context in which it is inscribed and the subjects that put it into action. Institutions do not precede instituent praxis, but they can be said to take form and develop within it.

What is proposed in theoretical terms was already widely anticipated in historical reality by the proliferation of institutional *dispositifs* that are external, and at times alternative, to the state order. From economics to law and politics, the order that once revolved around nation-states is entering into a dialectic of conflict with other institutions, public and private, global and local. Far from being neutralized, political conflict is situated at the heart of instituent praxis in a form that makes it hard to imagine a return to the old sovereignty of nation-states. In the long run, not even the current pandemic, with its threat of new lockdowns, will be able to stop this process of universalization, as attested to by the global spread of the virus and the confluence of responses to it, starting from the production of a vaccine.

The truth is that we have entered a biopolitical dimension that cannot be reduced to the sovereign paradigm. The growing importance given to living bodies, the classification of population segments based on age, gender, and health conditions, the increasingly close involvement between politics and medicine: all these signs of its diffusion point in this direction, brimming with opportunities and, along with them, risks. From this perspective, too, alongside and through individual choices, the function of institutions will assume a decisive importance in future society – on condition that they manage to cater to life affirmatively, re-establishing the apparently broken connection between institutions and movements. If movements only acquire strength and duration by becoming institutionalized, then institutions can only regain their creative power by mobilizing. The need to institute life has once again become the priority, in both senses: to vitalize institutions and to restore to life those instituent traits that propel it beyond mere biological matter.

August 2020

Notes

By Way of a Prologue

1 Hannah Arendt, *The Human Condition* (Chicago, IL: University of Chicago Press, 1958), p. 9.

I. The Eclipse

1 See his influential book, Franco Basaglia, ed., *L'Istituzione negata* (Milan: Baldini+Castoldi, 2013 [1970]).

2 Mary Douglas, *How Institutions Think* (London: Routledge and Kegan Paul, 1987).

3 See Yan Thomas, *Les opérations du droit*, ed. M.-A. Hermitte and P. Napoli (Paris: EHESS/Gallimard/Seuil, 2011). Thomas's essay on the institution of nature has been translated into Italian, along with a critical analysis by J. Chiffoleau and an essay by Michele Spanò, who also translated and edited the volume: *L'istituzione della natura* (Macerata: Quodlibet, 2020).

4 See Francesco Belvisi, "All'origine dell'idea di istituzione. Il concetto di 'persona ficta' in Sinibaldo

de' Fieschi," *Materiali filosofici*, no. 1, 1993, pp. 3–23.

5 See Pier Giovanni Caron, "Il concetto di 'institutio' nel diritto della Chiesa," *Il diritto ecclesiastico*, part 1, 1959, pp. 328–67.

6 See Paolo Napoli, "Ritorno a 'instituere': per una concezione materialistica dell'istituzione," in Francesco Brancaccio and Chiara Giorgi, eds., *Ai confini del diritto. Poteri, istituzioni e soggettività* (Rome: DeriveApprodi, 2017), pp. 77–88.

7 See Alain Guéry, "Institution. Histoire d'une notion et de ses utilisations dans l'histoire avant les institutionnalismes," *Cahiers d'économie politique*, no. 1, 2003, pp. 7–18.

II. The Return

1 See Marcel Mauss and Paul Fauconnet, *Sociologie*, in *Grande Encyclopédie*, vol. 30 (Paris, 1901), pp. 165–75; English translation, "Sociology," in *The Nature of Sociology*, trans. William Jeffrey, introduction by Mike Gane (New York: Durkheim Press/ Berghahn Books, 2005), pp. 1–30, here 10–11.

2 Ibid., p. 11.

3 Marcel Mauss and Henri Hubert, "Esquisse d'une théorie générale de la magie," in *Année Sociologique*, 1902–1903; English translation (based on the edition published in *Sociologie et anthropologie*, 1950): *A General Theory of Magic*, 2nd ed., trans. Robert Brain (London: Routledge, 2001), pp. 23–4.

4 Marcel Mauss, "Les techniques du corp," *Journal de Psychologie*, vol. 32, nos. 3–4, 1936; English translation, "Techniques of the Body," in Margaret Lock and Judith Farquhar, eds., *Beyond the Body*

Proper (Durham, NC: Duke University Press, 2007), pp. 50–68.

5 See Massimo Recalcati, "Il campo istituzionale tra Legge e desiderio: abbozzo per una teoria clinica dell'istituzione," *Almanacco di Filosofia e Politica*, no. 2, 2020, Mattia Di Pierro, Francesco Marchesi, and Elia Zaru (eds.), special issue on the institution, pp. 35–51.

6 See Maurice Hauriou, "La théorie de l'institution et de la fondation," *Cahiers de la nouvelle journée*, no. 4, 1925; English translation, "The Theory of the Institution and the Foundation: A Study in Social Vitalism," in *The French Institutionalists: Maurice Hauriou, Georges Renard, Joseph T. Delos*, trans. Mary Welling, edited by Albert Broderick, Introduction by Miriam Theresa Rooney (Cambridge, MA: Harvard University Press, 1970), pp. 93–124.

7 Santi Romano, *L'ordinamento giuridico*, edited by M. Croce (Macerata: Quodlibet, 2019 [1917–1918]), p. 43; English translation, *The Legal Order*, edited and translated by Mariano Croce (Abingdon, Oxon; New York: Routledge, 2017), p. 16.

8 See Santi Romano, *Lo Stato moderno e la sua crisi* (Milan: Giuffrè, 1967 [1909]).

9 For a rigorous reconstruction of the relationship between Husserl and Merleau-Ponty on the institution's subject, see Enrica Lisciani-Petrini, "Merleau-Ponty: potenza dell'istituzione," in *Discipline Filosofiche*, edited by Lisciani-Petrini and Massimo Adinolfi, no. 2, 2019, pp. 71–98. This is a special issue on the institution.

10 See Maurice Merleau-Ponty, "Institution in Personal

and Public History," in *In Praise of Philosophy and Other Essays*, trans. John Wild, James Edie, and John O'Neill (Evanston, IL: Northwestern University Press, 1970).

11 See Claude Lefort, "Sur la démocratie: le politique et l'institution du social," in *Textures*, no. 2/3, 1971, pp. 7–78.

12 See Mattia Di Pierro, *L'"esperienza del mondo" Claude Lefort e la fenomenologia del politico* (Pisa: Ets, 2020).

13 Of course, philosophical anarchism should not be confused with political anarchism. In this regard, see what Donatella Di Cesare writes in her "Anarchist postscript," in *The Political Vocation of Philosophy* (Cambridge: Polity, 2021), pp. 145ff.

14 See Claude Lefort, *Machiavelli in the Making*, trans. Michael B. Smith (Evanston, IL: Northwestern University Press, 2012).

15 For this interpretation of Machiavelli, see Francesco Marchesi, *Riscontro. Pratica politica e congiuntura storica in Nicolò Machiavelli* (Macerata: Quodlibet, 2017).

III. The Productivity of the Negative

1 For more on this topic, see Roberto Esposito, *Politics and Negation: For an Affirmative Philosophy*, trans. Zakiya Hanafi (Cambridge: Polity, 2019); and *Instituting Thought: Three Paradigms of Ontology*, trans. Mark William Epstein (Cambridge: Polity, 2021).

2 See Paul Ricoeur, "The Problem of the Foundation of Moral Philosophy," trans. David Pellauer, *Philosophy Today*, vol. 22, no. 3, 1978, pp. 175–92.

3 See Paul Ricoeur, "Le conflit: signe de contradiction ou d'unité?" in *Contradictions et conflits: Naissance d'une société*, Vol. 58 of *Semaines sociales de France* (Lyons: Chronique sociale de France, 1971), pp. 189–204.

4 Friedrich Nietzsche, *Beyond Good and Evil*, trans. Judith Norman (Cambridge: Cambridge University Press, 2003), p. 56.

5 Arnold Gehlen, *Man: His Nature and Place in the World* (1940), trans. Clare McMillan and Karl Pillemer, introduction by Karl-Siebert Rehberg (New York: Columbia University Press, 1988), p. 292.

6 Arnold Gehlen, *Urmensch und Spätkultur: Philosophische Ergebnisse und Aussagen* (1956) (Frankfurt: Klostermann, 2004); cited from the Italian translation: *L'uomo delle origini e la tarda cultura: Tesi e risultati filosofici*, ed. V. Rasini (Milan-Udine: Mimesis, 2016), p. 23.

7 See Theodor W. Adorno and Arnold Gehlen, "Ist die Soziologie eine Wissenschaft vom Menschen? Ein Streitgesprach (1965)," in Friedemann Grenz, *Adornos Philosophie in Grundbegriffen. Auflösung einiger Deutungsprobleme* (Frankfurt: Suhrkamp, 1974), pp. 224–51; cited from the Italian translation, "La sociologia è una scienza dell'uomo? Una disputa," in Theodor W. Adorno, Elias Canetti, and Arnold Gehlen, *Desiderio di vita. Conversazioni sulle metamorfosi dell'umano* (Milan-Udine: Mimesis), 1995, pp. 83–107.

8 Gilles Deleuze, *Desert Islands and Other Texts 1953–1974*, trans. Michael Taormina (New York: Semiotext(e), 2004), p. 20.

9 Cornelius Castoriadis, *The Imaginary Institution of Society* (1975) (Cambridge, MA: MIT Press, 1998).

IV. Beyond the State

1 James G. March and Johan P. Olsen, *Rediscovering Institutions: The Organizational Basis of Politics* (New York: The Free Press, 1989).

2 Gabriel A. Almond, "The Return to the State," *The American Political Science Review*, vol. 82, no. 3, 1988, pp. 853–74.

3 Douglass C. North, *Institutions, Institutional Change and Economic Performance* (Cambridge: Cambridge University Press, 1990).

4 On this topic, see Maria Rosaria Ferrarese, *Le istituzioni della globalizzazione* (Bologna: Il Mulino, 2000).

5 On the contradictions and opportunities of the European integration process, see Giuliano Amato and Ernesto Galli della Loggia, *Europa perduta?* (Bologna: Il Mulino, 2014).

6 As Biagio De Giovanni does in *L'ambigua potenza dell'Europa* (Naples: Guida, 2002), pp. 158ff.

7 See Mariano Croce, *Che cos'è un'istituzione* (Rome: Carocci, 2010), pp. 79ff.

8 Widar Cesarini Sforza, *Il diritto dei privati* (1929), ed. and with an essay by Michele Spanò (Macerata: Quodlibet, 2018), p. 112.

9 Ibid., p. 105.

10 See Niel MacCormick and Ota Weinberger, *An Institutional Theory of Law: New Approaches to Legal Positivism* (Dordrecht: Reidel, 1986); and Massimo La Torre, *Norme, istituzioni, valori. La*

teoria istituzionalistica del diritto (Rome-Bari: Laterza, 2002).

11 Cesarini Sforza, *Il diritto dei privati*, p. 104.

12 Ibid., p. 103.

13 See Gunther Teubner, "Fragmented Foundations: Societal Constitutionalism beyond the Nation State," in Petra Dobner and Peter Loughlin (eds.), *The Twilight of Constitutionalism* (Oxford: Oxford University Press, 2010), pp. 327–41. On Teubner, see Adalgiso Amendola, "Autopoiesi del sistema e autonomia dell'eccedenza," in Sandro Chignola (ed.), *Il diritto del comune. Crisi della sovranità, proprietà e nuovi poteri costituenti* (Verona: Ombre Corte, 2012), pp. 66–97.

14 See Aldo Schiavone, *The Invention of the Law in the West* (2005), trans. Jeremy Carden and Anthony Shugaar (Cambridge, MA: Harvard University Press, 2012).

15 Gunther Teubner, "Self-Subversive Justice: Contingency or Transcendence Formula of Law?" *The Modern Law Review*, vol. 72, no. 1, 2009, pp. 1–23.

16 On this topic, see Carlo Galli, *Sovranità* (Bologna: Il Mulino, 2019).

17 See the observations of Sandro Mezzadra and Brett Neilson in *The Politics of Operations: Excavating Contemporary Capitalism* (Durham, NC: Duke University Press, 2019), pp. 209ff.

18 See Jean Fourastié, *Les Trente Glorieuses, ou la révolution invisible de 1946 à 1975* [The glorious thirty years, or the invisible revolution of 1946 to 1975] (Paris: Fayard, 1979).

19 Étienne Balibar, *L'Europe, l'Amérique, la guerre* (Paris: La Découverte, 2003); Italian edition:

L'Europa, l'America, la guerra (Rome: Manifesto-
libri, 2003), pp. 111–17.

20 See Mario Tronti, *Dello spirito libero. Frammenti di
vita e di pensiero* (Milan: il Saggiatore, 2015).

21 See Pierre Dardot and Christian Laval, *Common:
On Revolution in the 21st Century*, trans. Matthew
MacLellan (London: Bloomsbury Academic, 2019).

V. Institutions and Biopolitics

1 Michel Foucault, *La volonté de savoir* (Paris:
Gallimard, 1976); English translation, *The History
of Sexuality vol. 1, The Will to Knowledge*, trans.
Robert Hurley (New York: Pantheon Books, 1978),
p. 137.

2 Foucault, *The Will to Knowledge*, p. 145.

3 Hannah Arendt, *The Human Condition* (Chicago,
IL: University of Chicago Press, 1958), p. 177.

4 Hannah Arendt, "Understanding and Politics," in
Essays and Understanding 1930–1954, ed. Jerome
Kohn (New York: Schocken Books, 1994), pp. 307–
27, here 320–1.

5 Ibid. For more on this topic, see Simona Forti,
Hannah Arendt tra filosofia e politica (Milan: Bruno
Mondadori, 2006).

6 See Pierre Legendre, *Sur la question dogmatique
en Occident. Aspects théoriques* (Paris: Fayard,
1999); Italian translation, *Il giurista artista della
ragione* (Turin: Giappichelli, 2000), p. 23. For
more by Legendre on this subject, see *De la Société
comme Texte. Linéaments d'une Anthropologie
dogmatique* (Paris: Fayard, 2001); [Italian translation, *Della società come testo. Lineamenti di
un'Antropologia dogmatica* (Turin: Giappichelli,

2005)]; *Sur la question dogmatique en Occident*, 2 vols. (Paris: Fayard, 1999 and 2006); and *Dogma: instituer l'animal humain. Chemins réitérés de questionnement* (Paris: Fayard, 2017).

7 Hannah Arendt, *On Revolution* (New York: Viking, 1963), p. 92.

8 On this topic, see Eligio Resta, *Diritto vivente* (Rome-Bari: Laterza, 2008).

9 See especially Eugen Ehrlich, *Grundlegung der Soziologie des Rechts* (Berlin: Duncker & Humblot, 1913); English translation, *Fundamental Principles of the Sociology of Law* (London and New York: Routledge, 2002).

10 See Sandro Chignola, ed. and introduction, *Il diritto del comune. Crisi della sovranità, proprietà e nuovi poteri costituenti* (Verona: Ombre Corte, 2012).

11 See Roberto Esposito, *Third Person: Politics of Life and Philosophy of the Impersonal*, translated by Zakiya Hanafi (Cambridge: Polity, 2012); *Two: The Machine of Political Theology and the Place of Thought*, trans. Zakiya Hanafi (New York: Fordham University Press, 2015); and Enrica Lisciani-Petrini, "Fuori della persona. 'L'impersonal' in Merleau-Ponty, Bergson e Deleuze," *Filosofia Politica*, no. 3, 2007, pp. 393–409.

12 Aldo Schiavone, *Eguaglianza. Una nuova visione sul filo della storia* (Turin: Einaudi, 2019), especially pp. 271ff; English translation, *The Pursuit of Equality in the West*, trans. Jeremy Carden (Cambridge, MA: Harvard University Press, 2022).

13 See Rita Fulco, *Soggettività e potere. Ontologia della vulnerabilità in Simone Weil* (Macerata: Quodlibet, 2020).

14 Émile Benveniste, "Relationships of Person in the Verb," in *Problems in General Linguistics*, trans. Mary Elizabeth Meek (Coral Gables, FL: University of Miami Press, 1970), pp. 205–15.

15 See Francesco Stoppa, *Istituire la vita. Come riconsegnare le istituzioni alla comunità* (Milan: Vita e Pensiero, 2014); Frédéric Worms, *Pour un humanisme vital. Lettres sur la vie, la mort et le moment présent* (Paris: Odile Jacob, 2019).

16 See the important book by Davide Tarizzo, *Life: A Modern Invention*, trans. Mark Willian Epstein (Minneapolis, MN: University of Minnesota Press, 2017).

17 Michel Foucault, *The Order of Things: An Archaeology of the Human Sciences* (New York: Vintage Books, 1970), p. 277.

Index

absolute monarchy 19, 20
Adorno, Theodor 47
alienation 42
Almond, Gabriel 57
American federalism 81, 82
American Revolution 83
ancestor worship 25
Ancien Régime 19, 20, 35
Anstalt 21–2
anthropocentrism 92–3
anti-institutional movements
    10, 12, 42
anti-state institutions 9–10
Arendt, Hannah vii, 1, 81–3,
    84
Aron, Raymond 31
authoritarian dimension of
    institutions 18, 21
Averroes 89

Balibar, Étienne 74
"bare life" 2, 91
Basaglia, Franco 11
Benjamin, Walter 2
Benveniste, Émile 89

Berger, Peter 11
Bergson, Henri 28, 42, 93
Bernard, Claude 28
Bichat, Xavier 91
biological life 1–2, 3, 77, 78,
    79, 83, 84
    opposition between
        institution and 83, 84
biopolitics 3, 8, 76–80, 83, 90,
    91–2, 94–5, 98
    coronavirus pandemic and 8,
        76–7, 98
    Foucauldian conception of
        91–2, 94–5
    immunological core of 77
biopower 79
bodily functions, institutional
    profile of 25–6
Bourdieu, Pierre 11
Bruno, Giordano 89
Buchanan, James M. 58

canon law 14, 15–16, 21, 96
capitalism 72
Castoriadis, Cornelius 52–3

Index

Cesarini Sforza, Widar 61–4
Christian canonists 14, 15–16
Christian doctrine of sacredness
    of life 3, 83–4
Christian political theology
    17
Cicero 17
citizenship 87
City of God (Augustine) 17
civilization, Freudian thesis of
    12
Coase, Ronald H. 58
coercive interpretation of
    institutions 12
the common 64, 68, 86
community 8, 64, 75, 77, 86
    communitas 3
    and immunity 8, 86
conflict 9, 35, 36, 37–8, 42, 43,
    67, 74, 98
conservatio vitae 3
conservative model of
    institution 10
constituent power vii, 13, 32,
    33, 54
constitution 85–6
constitutional experiments 73,
    74
contractualism 81
coronavirus pandemic 5–9, 58,
    75, 98
    biopolitical character of 8,
    76–7, 98
    miscalculations and failures
    to act 6
    response of institutions to 5,
    6–7, 8–9, 58, 77, 96
creativity
    of human nature 47
    of instituent praxis 52,
    98–9

Dardot, Pierre 75
deinstitutionalizing politics 56
Deleuze, Gilles 48, 49, 50, 89,
    93
democracy 35, 36, 48, 70, 74
    direct 43
    representative 43
denationalization 72
denaturalization 15–16
depoliticization 69–70, 72, 82,
    84
deregulation and
    deformalization 65
desistence 54
desocialization 8
destituent power 13
Deus institutor 16
dismantling of institutions 47
    see also anti-institutional
    movements
divine grace 22
divine right 20
divine will 16, 19, 96
Douglas, Mary 12
Duguit, Léon 27
Durkheim, Emile 23

ecological disasters 92–3
economists, institutionalist 58,
    59
Ehrlich, Eugen 85
élan vital 93, 95
European Union (EU) 61, 71,
    74
ex nihilo creation 32, 97
exoneration 45

Fascist corporatism 63–4
Fauconnet, Paul 23
Fieschi, Sinibaldo (Pope
    Innocent IV) 18

Index

financial markets 59, 60
Foucault, Michel 11, 78–80, 81,
  84, 89, 91–2, 94
French Revolution 20–1, 43,
  79, 83, 84
Freud, Sigmund 12, 93

Gehlen, Arnold 11, 44–6, 47,
  50, 53
geopolitics 57–8
Gerber, Carl 27
gift, institution of the 26–7
Goffman, Erving 11
Guéry, Alain 20
Gurvitch, Georges 30–1

Hauriou, Maurice 27–8
healthcare 8, 59, 88
Hegel, Georg Wilhelm Friedrich
  34, 41, 46
Heidegger, Martin 31, 42, 92
Hobbes, Thomas 3, 21, 37, 38,
  45, 48, 49
Hobbesian paradigm of order
  21, 23, 37, 81, 97
human fragility 44–5
human rights, violation of 67–8
Hume, David 49
Husserl, Edmund 31, 32

immunity 8, 68, 77, 86
  immune system 86–7
  immune device 87
the impersonal 33–4, 88–90, 94
instincts and institutions 48–52
instituent imaginary 52–5
instituent power 1, 16, 18, 37,
  82
instituent praxis 9, 17, 21, 24,
  26, 28, 31, 32, 33, 34, 35,
  40, 42–3, 44, 54–5, 56,

61, 65, 75, 77, 83, 88, 90,
  97, 98
creative character of 52
dialectical form 55
role of the negative 38,
  39–44, 45, 48, 49, 51–2
instituent thought vii, 33, 42,
  75, 94–5
instituting life 1–4, 5, 16, 76,
  90–5, 99
institutio vitae 3–4, 17, 24, 81,
  90
institution
  anti-state institutions 9–10
  authoritarian dimension 18,
    21
  bodily character 25
  closed and defensive
    conception of 11, 22, 96
  coercive dimension 12
  dismantling of 47
  dispositifs 11–12, 78, 98
  extra-state institutions 9
  genetic process 25
  linguistic role 26
  movements and 10–13, 30,
    42, 97, 98
  nature-institution relationship
    14–16, 26, 48, 49–50, 51
  primary task of 3, 46
  revitalization of 85 87–8, 90,
    98–9
  rigidification 10, 11, 12, 18,
    42, 54
  shift to modern concept of
    20–1
  of the social 34
  static notion of 9, 11, 14, 20,
    95
  tendency to equate with state
    institutions 9

Index

International Monetary Fund
60
Islamic fundamentalism 57
Italian institutionalism 8, 13,
66, 97

Jellinek, Georg 27
juridicity 65
justice
gap between rights and 68
law and 69, 70
subversive justice 66–71

Kelsen, Hans 85, 86

Laband, Paul 27
Laval, Christian 75
law
canon law 14, 15–16, 21, 96
collective 63–4
common law 64, 65, 70, 86,
87, 88
continental civil law 65
constituent function 66
formalism 64, 69
as immune subsystem of
social systems 86–7
impersonal law 88–90
and institutions 9, 27–31, 48,
51–2, 59–60
and justice 69, 70
legal formulas 47
legal positivism 24, 27
living law 85–6
natural law 16, 17
neutralizing role 68
organized and unorganized
30
and politics 48, 49, 61, 66
of private individuals 61–6,
70, 86, 89

public law 70, 86, 89
social character 2, 49, 62
Lefort, Claude 34
Legendre, Pierre 83
Leibnizian 69, 71
Lévi-Strauss, Claude 26
Levinas, Emmanuel 92
liberalism 52
life
"bare life" 2, 91
biological see biological life
and death 93–4
deinstitutionalized 92
dual character 1–2, 82–3, 91,
95
élan vital 93, 95
instituting life 1–4, 5, 16, 76,
90–5, 99
preservation of 3
will to life 92, 93
linguistic role of the institution
26
Lorenz, Konrad 12
Luckmann, Thomas 11
Luhmann, Niklas 66, 68, 86–7

Machiavelli, Niccolò 37–8, 74
March, James G. 56, 57
Marcianus 1
Marcuse, Herbert 11, 12
market uncertainty 59
marriage and property 50
Marx, Karl 41
Marxism 52, 56
Mauss, Marcel 23, 24, 26
Merleau-Ponty, Maurice 31,
32, 34
methodological individualism
51, 52, 56
Middle Ages 18–19
Montesquieu 81

Index

Mortati, Costantino 66
movements, institutions and
    10–13, 30, 42, 97, 98
natural law 16, 17
naturalism 46, 53
nature-institution relationship
    14–16, 48, 49–50, 51
Nazism 31, 47, 92
neoanarchism 43
neoclassical economics 58–9
neoinstitutionalism 57, 64
neoliberalism 72, 88
neomercantilism 72
Nietzsche, Friedrich 41, 44, 93
non-governmental organizations
    (NGOs) 7, 60, 70
North, Douglass C. 58, 59
novelty 32, 40, 82

objective spirit 34, 41
Olsen, Johan P. 56, 57
order 22, 30, 38, 62, 97, 98
    Hobbesian paradigm of 21,
        23, 37, 81, 97
    original and derivative 61
    prevalence of one over
        another 63
ordoliberalism 72
Orlando, Vittorio Emanuele
    28

Parsons, Talcott 21
personhood 34, 68, 88–9, 90,
    94
person-institutions 28
phenomenology 31–2
philosophical anthropology
    44–7, 50, 53
philosophy and the language of
    institution 31–4

pluralism, institutional 88
politics 34–8
    and the economy 72
    medicalization of 8
    political–theological polarity
        22
    and society 2, 10, 35, 55
    totalizing conception of 69,
        70
    see also biopolitics
post-state horizon 71–2
power 35–6, 63, 80
    biopower 79
    constituent power vii, 13, 32,
        33, 54
    destituent power 13
    instituent power 1, 16, 18,
        37, 82
    separation of powers
        principle 81–2
    sovereign power 29
private individuals, law of 61–6,
    70, 86, 89
privatization processes 65

racism 92
renationalization 72
"return to the state" 57
revitalization of institutions 85,
    87–8, 90, 98–9
Ricoeur, Paul 42
Roman jurists and juridical
    practice 1, 14, 15, 16, 17,
        53, 96
Roman model of institution
    14, 18
Roman tribune of the plebs 38
Romano, Santi 27, 28–30, 61,
    62, 66
Rousseau, Jean-Jacques 46, 81
Rubinelli, Lucia vii

Index

sacredness of life 3, 83–4
Saint-Just, Louis Antoine de vi
Sartre, Jean-Paul 11, 31
Savigny, Carl von 85
Schelling, Friedrich Wilhelm
    Joseph 89
Schiavone, Aldo 89
Schmitt, Carl 11, 21
Schopenhauer, Arthur 93
Schumpeter, Joseph A. 65
secularization 18, 84, 97
slavery 15
social contract 21, 49, 53
social engineering 47
social imaginary 52–5
sociology, institutions and
    23–7
Sohm, Rudolph 22
sovereignism 58, 71, 73
sovereignless institutions
    56–61
sovereignty 8, 18–22, 27, 29,
    30, 63, 71, 73, 78, 79, 82,
    98
  absolute 19, 27
  complexity and depth of 71
Spinoza, Baruch 64, 89
state of emergency 7, 77
state of exception 7, 77, 78

subjectivity 33, 68, 90
subversive justice 66–71

Tarde, Gabriel 28
technical prostheses, institutions
    as 45, 46, 47, 53
Teubner, Gunther 66, 69, 71
thanatopolitics 92, 93
thing-institutions 28
Thomas, Yan 14
"total institution" 11
total social fact 24
totalitarian society 35, 36
tyranny 48

utilitarianism 49

Varro, Marcus Terentius 17
Ventotene Manifesto 74
vitam instituere 1–4, 76, 83, 95

Weber, Max 21, 23, 41, 97
Weil, Simone 89
welfare
  construction 73
  reintroducing 88
Westphalian model, decline of
    57
World Trade Organization 60